Camera Movements That Confound Us

Camera Movements That Confound Us

Jonathan Rosenbaum

Sticking Place Books
New York

© Sticking Place Books 2025
© Jonathan Rosenbaum

www.stickingplacebooks.com

All rights reserved.
No part of this book may be reproduced, stored in or introduced into a retrieval system, or transmitted, in any form or by any means (electronic, mechanical, photocopying, recording or otherwise) without the written permission of the publishers, except in the case of brief quotations embodied in critical articles or reviews.

ISBN 978-1-942782-95-7

CONTENTS

Fifteen Prologues — 1

1. Clear Stepping Stones and Faltering Footsteps — 19

2. Hovering Over Landscapes — 37

3. Circular Reasoning in Cinema as Brainwashing and Live TV Dramas — 47

4. F. W. Murnau and The Poetics of Delirium — 59

5. Perpetual Motion in Altman's *The Long Goodbye* — 63

6. Early Ozu: Camera Movement as Inspection — 67

7. Alain Resnais and the Art of Disavowal — 73

8. Four Dynamic Metaphysical Movements — 85

9. I Love the Rhythm in a Riff: Hitchcock's Pans and Collective Authorship — 97

A Non-Conclusive Epilogue (*Cuadecuc, Vampir*) — 111

Acknowledgements — 117

Index — 119

FIFTEEN PROLOGUES

1

These are the notes of an uneasy, ambivalent spectator. But of course context changes everything. Sometimes a camera movement is simply a storytelling tool allowing one to pass from A to B in a fictional narrative—accompanying, following, or ignoring the paths taken by others onscreen. But it's also a tool trained on us and our predilections for non-fictional fantasies as well as fictional ones. So the movement to be considered is not only the camera's but our own, real or imagined (and most often both).

Please consider what follows a nonexhaustive assembly of literary skirmishes from me and a few valued writers, not a finished argument to be fished out of the imbroglio, waiting to be dried off and snugly named, cosseted, and civilized like a yowling brat. I'd rather deepen and expand the mysteries involved and make them more user-friendly than pretend to resolve them, even if they still keep me awake at night.

Please also bear in mind that when I quote myself, I'm usually speaking from the vantage point of a re-reader having a skeptical conversation with my younger self, not the same person who wrote the passage in question. And when I quote others at length, this is either because they say things I'd like to have said or because they say things

I'd like to counter or refute, and sometimes both reasons are operative. Like a confounding camera movement, the distances between then and now or here and there aren't always smooth sailing, but I've come to regard bumps in the road as corrective reality lessons.

2

A camera movement that confounds us, whether it does this deliberately or accidentally, resembles some of the best as well as worst of William Faulkner's purple passages, jabbering stretches of babble that always defeat us with the vehemence of their cold fury, regardless of whether they register as poetry or as parody or as intractable prose or simply as pure hostile aggression.

Consider the second sentence of Faulkner's *Pylon* (1935), about a pair of boots seen by a character in a shop window:

> Slantshimmered by the intervening plate they sat upon their wooden pedestal in unblemished and inviolate implication of horse and spur, of the posed countrylife photographs in the magazine advertisements, beside the easelwise cardboard placard with which the town had bloomed overnight as it had with the purple-and-gold tissue bunting and the trodden confetti and broken serpentine… the same lettering, the same photographs of the trim vicious fragile aeroplanes and the pilots leaning upon them in gargantuan irrelation as if the aeroplanes were a species of esoteric and fatal animals not trained or tamed but just for the instant inert, above the neat brief legend of name and accomplishment or perhaps just hope.*

---

* William Faulkner, *Novels 1930-1935* (Library of America, 1985), 779.

Like so much of Faulkner's furious prose, this is compulsive and relentless movement representing stasis, swirling rhetoric around a still object or objects whose very inertness seems to unleash the cascading verbosity.

Whatever the gesture's social impact, and whether the camera's movement is driven by happy foretaste or by sullen fear, it evokes a cosmic absence and creepy silence that not even all the junk and noise in the world can pretend to fill (which doesn't mean that we don't keep trying)—an absence that the camera either penetrates or backs away from, in response to the aching lack. As Faulkner's yawning crevices remind us, the gaps are ours to fill, meaning that who we are helps to determine what we see and hear.

3

Camera movements rarely ask us to think. A rising crane exulting over a particular scene is a form of mythmaking, not a way of thinking about a given subject. As Daniel Morgan (in Prologue #13, below) rudely yet accurately points out, what we call camera movements are often mythical objects for cinephiles to play with that owe much of their allure to the fantasies we spin around them—or maybe it's the fantasies they spin around us. (It always takes two to tango.) Even when camera movements dutifully and mechanically follow characters walking or running or dancing and are not supposed to be noticed more than incidentally, there is something expressionistic as well as metaphysical about their employment, the way they seem to direct our attentions by nudging us the way that art does and not the way that nature does.

These camera movements can offer adventurous escapes of varying kinds, from thoughtful ruminations, judicious escape clauses, to irresponsible and irresistible twinges of a child's awe and flights of fancy away from boring reality.

4

"There are neither good nor bad subjects," Flaubert declared in one of his letters. "One might almost establish an axiom, looking from the point of view of pure art, to the effect that there is no subject; style itself being an independent manner of seeing things."* This is typical of the way we misread film style. Cinephiles discussing camera movements often treat them as forms of pure art, without subject matter—an absurd notion, because if it weren't for the subjects kindled in our brains and lives by some of the camera movements of Murnau, Renoir, Ophüls, Welles, Kubrick, Altman, Tarkovsky, Muratova, Akerman, Tarr and Weerasethakul, and the diverse emotions they can evoke and perpetuate, it couldn't function as Art (or art) in the first place. Which is another way of suggesting that art without a subject ultimately adds up to art without an audience. Flaubert ultimately priced himself out of the market, although this hasn't prevented generations of grateful academics and freelance commentators from taking over his expenses.

This is all hypothetical and therefore theoretical. Be forewarned that sick critiques of sick behavior are quickly and easily transformed for profit into ad-like celebrations, specialties of the marketplace and its momentary amusements (to be is to sell, or to be sold), corruptions that we invariably buy into whenever we decide to watch movies.

Whether we keep on consuming more and more of it or it starts consuming more and more of us, the sound of all this mastication is deafening thanks to all the clatter, the cacophony of cutlery and plates and chewing, reminding us of the proximity of ears to teeth.

---

* John Charles Tarver, *Gustave Flaubert As Seen In His Works and Correspondence* (Archibald Constable, 1894), 141.

5

Not just camera movement so much as instant transport from one thought or feeling to another, the impatient rush of narrative itself. A camera and a set of tracks provide an imperfect vehicle for carrying us between thoughts or emotions, but does this sentence and this clause do the job any better? I wonder… and wander, each "w" getting softly crushed underfoot as I proceed blindly but compulsively forward, the percussive flutter of individual lives and pages pushing me ahead.

As I understand it, camera movement involves a displacement of a viewer's attention within the same nexus of time and space that we call a shot, and a confounding camera movement is one that disrupts and/or challenges our viewing and thinking habits, including our senses of what a shot and narrative flow might be. Some of these disruptions and challenges are uncanny, but by no means all of them. Writing as someone with limited practical and physical knowledge of what moving a camera entails, I will generally concentrate on effects rather than technical means, so my appraisals of uncanny camera movements in Carl Dreyer's final half-dozen features is more a matter of how they make me feel than a matter of pinpointing what they actually do and how they achieve their uncanny effects. Dreyer is arguably cinema's supreme master of uncanny camera movement, but a significant part of his mastery lies in his ability to conceal certain parts of his methodologies so that we seemingly respond to his stories and characters more than to his techniques.

Consequently, the camera's complete encirclement of Johannes and Maren (both seated) in *Ordet* while they remain positioned either frontally or in profile, with Maren lit more brightly than Johannes throughout the scene, is a "miracle" that we're meant to accept without being aware that we're doing so. Whether or not this was made possible by a rotating set is irrelevant to the scene's focus, which is the characters' conversation about Inger, Maren's mother and Johannes' sister-in-law. This suggests that Dreyer is getting us to accept one miracle as preparation for accepting another, Inger's resurrection, soon afterwards.

6
Having served as Mehrnaz Saeed-Vafa's camera assistant on her essay film about Frank Lloyd Wright's Stanley Rosenbaum house in Alabama where I grew up (*A House is Not a Home: Wright or Wrong*, 2020), I've executed a few camera movements myself, sometimes with the aid of a rented wheelchair in which Saeed-Vafa sat with a video camera while I pushed her around. Using a wheelchair is of course what Jean-Luc Godard and Raoul Coutard did on *Breathless* (1960), but the camera movements I regarded as models for my own mostly came from Sacha Vierny's in *Last Year in Marienbad* (1961) or (when I pushed Mehrnaz in one direction while she panned her camera in another direction) from some of the talkies of Carl Dreyer. But the coordination between my movements and Saeed-Vafa's didn't necessarily register as the same movements because context (such as how she edited the shots) changes everything. So one might say that the camera movements seen by viewers of her films are singular expressions of multiple acts performed by Saeed-Vafa and myself with the aids of camera, projector, laptop, wheelchair, and viewers — many intermediate movers contributing via some form of teamwork to what is perceived as a singular act and impulse, a singular movement.

Why should the rolling movement of a camera/wheelchair down a narrow hallway matter more than the flickering movement between each film frame of its progress? Simply because the movement between frames is meant to be experienced without being noticed, whereas the movement down a narrow hallway is meant to be both noticed *and* experienced. (The difference between handheld movements and those of a camera on a tripod are often matters of relative bumpiness versus relative smoothness, commonly affecting how and how much we're thinking about the camera as a player in the action.)

This combination of voluntary and involuntary participation is part of what's confounding about what Alexandre Astruc once called the "*caméra-stylo.*" The very act of writing with a pen might imitate the activity of a dance, but the experience of filmgoing is partly that of *being* danced, or *being* written by the *caméra-stylo* — a creepy form of engagement, of being engaged.

7

Camera movements are invariably linear even when their lines run in circles, but this doesn't mean that every line has to progress logically or rationally, and this book is mainly concerned with occasions when logic and rational thoughts are missing, diverted, or just plain elusive. Camera movements sometimes offer momentary escape from plot points and other enforced itineraries and gradual inductions into various independent or tangential erotic and sensual pursuits.

8

> That banal little word "and" leaves us in a place somewhere between comprehension and mystery.

Fintan O'Toole happens to be discussing (in "No Comfort," *The New York Review of Books*, June 6, 2024) the unsettling effect of an operation in a very literary form of surgery — an operation performed repeatedly by

Shakespeare in his greatest tragedies and in some of their most resonant lines.

O'Toole also appears to be describing what certain confounding camera movements do to us. It's a slightly over-the-cliff sort of feeling produced by Shakespeare violently mating two words that don't ordinarily seem to be on speaking terms with one another, a rude matchup of a blind date that almost feels like a sadistic assertion of power designed to shake us all out of our protective complacencies and orbits, including those very words that Shakespeare forced together after yanking each one out of its respective and protective shell.

On the other hand, the words "slightly" and "almost" in the previous paragraph function as pivots that allow the mated words to slide into the sex and orgasms unleashed on our premises—that is, on our own property and with our own ideas. So our creative interactivity is part of what makes the movement artistic.

9

Sometimes the whole point of an uncomfortable camera movement is to take us somewhere—think of the Haunted House theme-park ride in Disneyland—and sometimes the overarching motivation is simply to keep us moving, no matter what or where or when. Either way, it's more of a command than an invitation, a directive to let yourself be swept off your feet or inserted into a vehicle meant to be driven by some form of narrative if you're a storyteller, some form of portraiture if you're a painter, and some kind of music or theater if you're a composer/performer/writer, and/or a listener/spectator.

Aren't we all of us all of these things much of the time, even though we're loathe to admit it? We tend to believe in the fantasies that we help to weave ourselves more than the jolts of reality that are imposed on us. As I've suggested elsewhere, with a nudge from Faulkner's

Light in August ("Memory believes before knowing remembers"), (our) imaginations believe more than (our) knowing constructs, especially when we're dreaming or watching a movie. We remember the journalistic simplifications and Hollywood riffs about the news while forgetting the less tidy and less camera-ready details that may come closer to the truth but are harder to recognize and classify because they aren't so snugly *placed*.

The uncomfortable part can be an unexpected punchline or a lingering aftereffect, a sudden bump in the road or a twist in the prose. Whatever it turns out to be, we're stuck with it because it also commonly delivers the final chord, which sometimes becomes the final discord.

Discomfort can only sneak or crawl into a given movement or space evoking emptiness. (Yet how can it really be empty when we're filling that space and participating in that movement?) Walking, standing still, and snoozing are all discouraged because they tend to produce boredom by adhering to familiar conventions and formulas. To move uncomfortably sometimes means to slip and slide, creep and hide, eluding the cookie-cutters that insist on repetitive patterns.

But sometimes the basic reason (i.e., pleasure) for moving a camera is simply to advance a narrative, push it forward, either filling in with environmental details or with flirty suggestions of possible adventures to come. In other words, telling a story—the *caméra-stylo* kept active and healthy by gobs of ink and jolts of electricity, whether they're pursuing a sentence or a sequence, filling a page or a shot, a thought or a feeling, an idea or a room, sometimes even all these things at once.

10

"Are we there or not?" is the question proposed by every movie, always requiring multiple and contradictory responses.

11 (a political digression—or extension)
Over the course of film history, a surprising number of artistic discoveries and subversions are derived from juxtaposing supposed fiction with supposed non-fiction—shotgun marriages that play with our reflexes regarding what we assume we're watching, hearing, and/or appraising or evaluating. Camera movements sometimes perform and enact these juxtapositions, whether they're connecting fictional characters to "real" locations or contriving to convert a documentary spectacle that is found into a created narrative that is followed. Even though it might be argued that (1) all films are fictional, even (and maybe even especially) when we receive them as reportage, and (2) all films are documentaries, even when we treat them like made-up stories. The human will that moves a camera encourages us to see that our responses are similarly willed and mutable, theoretically allowing us to believe in made-up stories and disbelieve whatever evidence might be shoved in front of us. Getting politicians to behave and perform like characters in comic strips or Hollywood movies or TV commercials or sitcoms obviously helps this process along.

My personal definition of "youth": the time when I could still believe that the evening news and brassy Hollywood movies were distinct and dissimilar entities and activities, not two versions of the same ongoing boondoggle. (All things considered, *The Tonight Show* and *Star Wars* are reverse sides of the same showbiz coin.) When I browsed my spam during the summer of 2024, I read stuff like "Biden is Fuming" or "Trump is Boiling Over" or "Kamala Harris takes a 'gotcha' question on her record as a prosecutor and just shreds it" or "Jon Stewart SHUTS DOWN MSNBC & CNN for Biased Reporting"—all essentially fictional movie pitches complete with obligatory violent imagery for all of us, the hysterical ten-year-olds being addressed as the ideal spectators. (To celebrate its special talent for working both sides of the street, the *New York Times* headlined its weekly dialogue between Gail Collins and Bret Stephens on January 28, 2025, "Trump Explodes Out of the Gate," licking its chops over this movielike flourish, and Stephens himself says, "Like it or not, you and I and the rest of America are locked into this movie theater for the next four years. Pass the popcorn.")

Yet these strident pitches also read as if they were written by and for robots, offering essentially the same programing cues, echoing the same formulas, clichés, and lies, and thus sounding artificial because it's presumed that we prefer it that way, all jazzed up. But if our TV news is now being shaped and delivered like our advertising, it becomes difficult at times to determine whether a camera movement is a simple narrative tool or a lyrical form of decoration. TV ads tend to favor camera movement, but now many of the so-called news broadcasts favor swooping camera moves across studio sets that aim to evoke the vitality of the ads.

How can you "shred" a "gotcha" question? It's easy to pretend that you're doing something superficially cinematic, making bold gestures, especially if you can do it to music, turning it into a dance performed inside a vacuum. Camera movements are excursions that often depend on music to contextualize how we should feel about them. So let's shift the blame whenever possible and insist that algorithms, not people, are the cause of our helpless confusion, a confusion that only coincidentally happens to be profitable to other people.

MSNBC's coverage of the Democratic National Convention in August 2024, which often used camera movements to suggest giddy convergences, proposed an impromptu mix of Ed Sullivan and Rachel Maddow pooling their bombastic talents to voice and coin their superlatives ("We've got a really big show tonight" is the favorite phrase of both impresarios), the all-star allure of a sporting event or the Oscars overtaking any effort to separate thought and politics from deliberately nonserious entertainment and advertising. Our hopeful legacy cast in the form of brassy circus acts and church celebrations, all pursued as worthy excuses for teenage exuberance.

The potential deceit of every camera movement found in the news is its insistence that it's only being factual, not rhetorical, even though its power is to evoke, excite, spin and/or make spin, not really to instruct us about anything.

And what is being evoked? Ads growing into trailers for other ads that fill our movie screens, filling our eyes and ears with false promises in the forms of directives, arrows inspired by what artificial intelligence has determined to be our deepest (i.e., most profitable) desires. Or maybe these are just stretches of Internet jive written by people who want to emulate and imitate robots, as so many of us already seem to be doing, thus executing a chilly, disdainful pan from MSNBC soundbites about narcissistically "living in these truly *historical* times" (my italics) to Hollywood cartoon versions of American History as dreamed up by Disney, Ford, De Mille, or Spielberg (e.g., the TV news label "War in the Gulf," complete with desert logo and brassy music). What seems confounding about this pan is that it seems to be only pretending to adopt a cynical stance towards what it secretly condones and even cherishes, because the movement of the camera is usually celebratory, not defeatist. And the pan from one version of nowhere to another, from neo-historical narcissism (We Are the World and We Are History) to theme-park history (The World Has Always Belonged To Us, at least for the price of a ticket) isn't a switch of substance or even style but just a change in lighting to make the boondoggle a bit more digestible, like a shared joke. (Aren't We Something "Special"? Particularly Because We're All in This Mess "Together"?) Making it a camera movement greased by the butter of an ersatz alliance between heart and home—ersatz because heart and home are equally absent, drummed out by the profit motive that rules the media, strategically misread as positive energy.

Or is it a defeatist movement, a nihilistic retreat from heart and home alike? Whatever we choose, we're opting for another movie—not another "slice of life" but what Alfred Hitchcock playfully juxtaposed it with, what he called a "slice of cake." Camera movement as sensual invitation and discovery versus the kind of jive calculated to close you down or at least shut you out as well as off (bad life, bitter cake, lousy cinema or ad copy, always in italics). A cowardly form of departure, in any case, designed to resemble a holiday vacation. But even if you're buying a round-trip ticket for your favorite theme-park ride, you aren't really budging an inch. That's what we mean by entertainment. All that's really moving is you and the merchandise, carried along by money and tears and music, only secondarily by cameras. Yet context, of course, changes everything.

The Yankee association of art with money—whereby operas and symphony orchestras are thought to belong to the same sort of class posture and posturing as a taste for brie and cappuccino—helps to explain how and why the term "beautiful camera movement" inevitably conjures up piles of moolah, the sheer expense of laying down smooth tracks or executing ever lighter and smoother pans rather than the shakier handheld gyrations and fumblings of working-class employees trying to fulfill their bosses' obscure game plans. No getting around it: what we usually mean by expressive camera movements, from Mamoulian or Minnelli, Muratova or Mizoguchi, Malick or Mankiewicz, are matters involving money that benefit from lavish spending power, with the sheer MGM ritziness of an orchestral Miklós Rózsa score (like the one commissioned by Alain Resnais for *Providence*), a lapful of Technicolor, and a few swooping cranes dutifully ready to back up and italicize all its bold assertions. Creepy camera movements in these climes often partake of the Gothic, in one way or another, beckoning us to fall into some version of the dark unknown. This is the Gothic path taken by many of the mysterious camera moves in *Citizen Kane*, *The Magnificent Ambersons*, *Rebecca*, *Gilda*, *The Earrings of Madame de…*, *Last Year at Marienbad* and *Providence*, all of which plunge us into horrible family or proto-family secrets. Victorian repression is always one of the uncredited auteurs in the studio's herd of rewriters, and almost every creepy camera movement to be found in this jungle of carbon copies reflects its imprint.

The persistence of liberal anchorpeople in telling us that we're living in "historic" times (which optimistically presupposes a future that could make both the present and ourselves doubly meaningful) seems to consider "historical" a euphemism for "hysterical," which arguably serves as a more fitting adjective for our era. Bearing this euphemism in mind, it's worth stressing that mysterious camera movements are often hysterical but seldom historical, suggesting that they aren't mysteries awaiting solutions but experiences meant to be undergone and then absorbed and/or forgotten but never "understood." Which is another way of saying that a confounding camera movement isn't a question but it's one way of getting us to ask a question.

13

It's a truism that the first step in any real education is the discovery of one's ignorance. My own ignorance about camera movement begins with a common form of self-deception that is usefully spelled out by Daniel Morgan in his recent book *The Lure of the Image: Epistemic Fantasies of the Moving Camera*.* (If, like me until very recently, you're ignorant about what "epistemic" means, it's an adjective relating to knowledge or to the degree of its validation.)

As Morgan puts it in his first chapter:

> The logic of the camera-eye, the sense that the way we look at the world of a film proceeds through the look of a camera, that we are with the camera when it moves through the world, is the most dominant and important account of the moving camera… Yet the logic behind this fundamental idea is deeply flawed. To put it bluntly, we are not within the world of the film, seeing it from the perspective of the camera, that is an illusion… At the same time, however, and importantly, even though we recognize this, even though we *know* that we cannot be in the world of the film with the camera, we *feel* it to be the case.†

Like many other cinephiles, I've been living this feeling-versus-thinking contradiction for most of my life, and because certain feelings as well as (often imperfect) thoughts are aroused by camera movements, I can't simply ignore the former for the sake of the latter. Indeed, all films are fantasies, and if we tend to adopt the fantasy cited by Morgan whenever we watch a camera movement, this only matches our fantasy that we're watching a continuous reality (or a continuous premise of a reality) and not a succession of separate frames, contingent on the related fantasy that cameras can "watch" or "look"

---

* California, 2021.
† Ibid., pp. 4-5.

rather than simply record whatever happens to be in front of them. Turning cameras into watchers or lookers is really just another way of surrendering to the billionaires who want us to believe that cameras are robots, i.e., perfectible people, not unthinking machines.

14

The fact is that we tend to live according to faulty metaphors and inexact labels whereby brown people are often routinely misidentified as either white or black, military occupations can sometimes be misdescribed as wars (as in the so-called Gulf War), and censorship can be attributed to diverse forms of tyranny that systematically exclude capitalism—to cite only three examples among dozens that thrive in our transcendental culture. In a 1947 essay ("America the Beautiful: The Humanist in the Bathtub"), the usually brilliant political and literary commentator Mary McCarthy asserts that "The strongest argument for the unmaterialistic character of American life is the fact that we tolerate conditions that are, from a materialistic point of view, intolerable."* And in her 1981 book *Ideas and the Novel*, she inadvertently proves just how American she is by asserting that a film "cannot have a spokesman or chorus character as in a stage play; that function is assumed by the camera, which is inarticulate"†— a little bit like saying that a poem can't have a dumb pencil, a pencil that can't even utter a syllable. "And the absence of spokesmen in the films we remember," she adds—thereby banishing from our memories significant films by Bresson, Cocteau, Godard, Sternberg, and Welles—"shows rather eerily that with the cinema, humanity has found a narrative medium that is incapable

---

* *A Bolt from the Blue and Other Essays*, edited by A. O. Scott (New York Review Books, 2002), 230.
† I didn't keep this book after reviewing it, but can cite my published review as the source: https://jonathanrosenbaum.net/2023/08/mccarthys-law-review-of-ideas-and-the-novel/.

of thought."* Incapable of eliciting thought from Mary McCarthy, in any case.

But once we concede that the people who use cinema, cameras, and projectors are capable of thoughts, and that sometimes they can think of ways to use cameras and projectors and cinema to produce other thoughts, then it stands to reason that cinema, cameras, and projectors can sometimes help us to think.

The uses of subjective, first-person camera movement in Robert Montgomery's *Lady in the Lake* and the beginning of Delmer Daves' *Dark Passage* (both in 1947) may not generate much thought from us, but Rouben Mamoulian's use of it at the start of his *Dr. Jekyll and Mr. Hyde* back in 1931 is far more thought-provoking because it forces us to consider our relation to Jekyll's theory about Man's psychological duality not only before he turns into Mr. Hyde but much earlier, before he looks in a mirror on his way to give a medical lecture about man's duality and shows us that Jekyll looks a lot like Fredric March. Much later, a sudden camera movement in his lab connecting his gaze to a human skeleton and then darting back to him before he takes his magic potion is even more thought-provoking, as are diverse momentary returns to subjective camera to show us what the world (including Hyde himself) looks like to Mr. Hyde. So cameras can certainly provoke and guide our thoughts even if they can't think for themselves.

In the interests of honoring both thoughts and feelings, cinema and literature, ideas and spaces, I've structured this book to reflect different and even contradictory methods of describing camera movements—what they do and how they manage to land in our sensibilities. Nine chapters which can be read in any order preceded by fifteen prologues. If I could address Mary McCarthy's ghost today, I'd ask her to regard this book as a collection

---

* Ibid.

of thoughts—some connected, some disconnected—but not any thoughts coming from unthinking cameras or inarticulate cinemas. I also regard this as an undeclared anthology of many voices, my own in conversation with others like McCarthy and Morgan. If I sometimes choose to ignore Morgan's sensible objections as well as McCarthy's less sensible ones, this is because it offers me more options, more license to travel in a wider world encompassing fantasy as well as documentary that allows for certain silences between the lectures, like the strategic spaces/pauses delivered between phrases in piano solos by Count Basie, Thelonious Monk, and Ahmad Jamal.

Frank Lloyd Wright called television "chewing gum for the eyeballs." But media's digital junkie feed is more like an injection than any form of exercise, however abject or mechanical. It's like taking all your lessons from machines, waiting to be activated by logarithms (which is code for stupid billionaires). A machine, after all, can execute a camera movement far more smoothly and heroically than any faltering, blustering human, so that's what we've chosen to honor and obey.

1
CLEAR STEPPING STONES AND FALTERING FOOTSTEPS

Stepping stones are for walking and for crossing creeks and streams—not for thinking, though we may wind up with a stray thought or two once we've reached the other side. Moreover, passing from the physical to the metaphysical is the most common way a camera movement can confound us. While stepping from one stone to another, we might be reminded of drumbeats or heartbeats, but one thing these seeming repetitions also offer is the possibility of uncanny twists or blips causing us to slip, slide, stumble, and fall. So we'd better watch out. Oblivion awaits us if we should trip or falter.

Oblivion, for that matter, is the implied destination and/or backdrop of every Howard Hawks picture—namely the emptiness and doom that's lurking on the periphery of every mainstream Hawks character and set, every location, network, or cozy interior, thus constantly facing the premise and perhaps even the promise of splashy, cold obliteration. And usually without even bothering to move the camera much, if at all, establishing the limits of one's vision by other means. In any case, the mainstream discourse of even an "invisible" stylist like Hawks always flirts with the possibility of disaster, so it's reasonable to assume that unpredictable, expressive camera movements can function a little bit like death wishes. (It's always been clear that Hawks hated suicidal characters in other people's movies because he was perpetually afraid of becoming one of those misfits himself. Being obsessed with normality usually means guarding against the many possibilities of abnormality, commonly and misleadingly personified by the wolf at one's door rather than in one's mirror.)

I think one can define every Hawks feature as some sort of horror movie that involves aging (*Monkey Business*), mutilation (*The Big Sky*, *Red Line 7000*), mortality (*Scarface*, *Only Angels Have Wings*, *Land of the Pharaohs*), or simply the encroaching void (all of the above) — all the supposedly nasty stuff that most people prefer not to think about while bathing in the mainstream. That's why the Hawksian universe always includes an enclave of *refusées* clinging to one another during a never-ending storm, a cozy kind of good-fellow togetherness that usually precludes much thought. Creating automatic empathy for every other creature inside your own nest plus an automatic fear of, and scorn for, anyone stupid enough to occupy any other nest is quintessentially Hawksian, so that we forget we're watching a movie and refer to what we're doing as relaxation, i.e., not thinking. So we can see where and what Mary McCarthy's thoughtlessness is coming from.

I'm not referring to the camera movements following characters as they move though the adjoining rooms of Sterling Hayden's flat in Stanley Kubrick's *The Killing* (1956), with the camera in effect tracking outside the set to follow characters inside the set, because this movement is dictated by narrative momentum, a shared desire to pursue characters and a plot — not exactly a physical journey meant to be experienced as such but arguably something closer to a metaphysical shortcut. Our lives, our thoughts, and especially our movies are filled with many such sweet-cheat shortcuts. But uncanniness, a form of dispossession, suggests that one can't even be sure what "this" is, meaning that no one can confidently claim it unless it's a defined object to be pointed at.

Nor am I thinking about the locomotion, call it the slidewalk, of Jack Nicholson's son riding his tricycle in Kubrick's *The Shining* (1980) as he foot-pedals his way through a cavernous empty hotel because even though his feet are involved in the forward movement, footsteps per se are absent. The thrust of most camera movements in Kubrick, including the slow, backward zooms in *Barry Lyndon* (1975), are seamless excursions precluding footsteps, and the same can be said of the 360-degree turnarounds of Carl Dreyer (in *Ordet*), Alfred Hitchcock (in *Vertigo*, possibly recalling the example of *Ordet* by keeping our view of James Stewart and Kim Novak mostly frontal), and Brian De Palma and Paul Schrader (in their countless *Vertigo* pastiches). It's worth thinking about what makes the circular spins of Dreyer and Hitchcock uncanny and those of De Palma and Schrader something closer to redundant footnotes and/or the pissing of dogs to mark their own property, their folksy way of declaring "This is mine" even though it once belonged to Hitchcock (or maybe to Dreyer having inspired Hitchcock). Snugness and smugness of this kind reflect Yankee pride at its dumbest as well as its finest, in one happy consumerist glut.

Parenthetically, it's remarkable how a film such as *Vertigo*, seemingly the most respected item in the Hitchcock canon—and a film that jumped over four decades *in Sight and Sound's* global critics poll from seventh (1982) to fourth (1992) to second (2002) to first place (2012)—has a central premise that depends on a ridiculous contrivance, its hero (James Stewart) being fooled into believing that the heroine (Kim Novak) has leapt to her death from a church tower. It's a premise that would immediately evaporate if he attended her inquest and discovered that another woman fell to her death, but it seems that the film's honoring of this hero's obsession allows it to leapfrog over this loophole without a moment's doubt or pause. Maybe it's the power of the film's focusing on his footsteps racing up the stairs of the church tower and their compulsive rhythms that overwhelm the reasoning power of most viewers. Consciously or not, it may be the power of cinema to defy causality and even reality that's being applauded.

Who knows why we're so susceptible to being fooled? The stepping stones I have in mind turn our eyes into surrogates for our feet, and we're so transfixed by the passing scenery that we might even forget that we're walking or running. By the same token, it's usually in the interests of the Hollywood studios to keep us ignorant of who we are and what we're doing while we're taking those steps.

By contrast, the seemingly gratuitous 360-degree camera spins around studio sets on cable TV news, shows that are not supposed to have any auteurs, only anchors, seem to be assertions of presence and vitality, "This is all there is"—our smooth machinery delivering the news to us, too intense and urgent to allow us to turn away or even to catch our breaths. This is arguably the rationale of the camera's movements in Hitchcock's *Rope* (1948)—to capture some of the immediacy of live theater and its employments of "real time."

There's a comparable urgency to Rainer Werner Fassbinder's spectacular 720-degree tracking shot in *Martha* (1974), the camera encircling the title heroine (Margit Carstensen) and her husband-to-be, Helmut Salomon (Karlheinz Böhm) when they first encounter one another on a street in Rome, immediately after her father's death. It's tempting to ascribe this kind of high style—also apparent at the banquet back in Germany, where Martha first gets introduced to her sadistically abusive husband-to-be—to personal factors. Fassbinder had a particular investment in this material that his collaborators have noted, including cinematographer Michael Balhaus and Karlheinz Böhm in Juliane Lorenz's *Chaos as Usual: Conversations About Rainer Werner Fassbinder*.* Lorenz reports that Fassbinder consciously based the portrayal of Helmuth Salomon on his own father, and even dressed like his father in conservative neckties, shirts, and suits throughout the film's production—an association that seems echoed by Helmuth surfacing magically as a kind of döppelganger-replacement for Martha's own father immediately after the latter's death. Thus the 720-degree camera rotation around their first encounter amounts to a cinematic counterpart to italics. And Fassbinder's parody of bourgeois marriage as a sadomasochistic charade is a slimy self-portrait whose articulated pleasure via camera movement also becomes an indictment of the audience for sharing that pleasure.

Regarding the list that follows: as in *Martha*, footsteps are not necessarily shown, but the height and position of the camera assume them in any case—one camera movement and at least one off-balance gasp per film title, all uncanny trips into the unknown governed by the activity of feet in motion, leading God knows where. (Circus music starts here, as in a TV commercial.) Nine of these feetward forays follow. More precisely, all of them relate to walking in one way or another, literally or referentially.

1.
I can't say if the uncanny camera movement near the beginning of F. W. Murnau's masterpiece *Sunrise* (1927) is the first one I ever saw and recognized as such, but it makes a convenient starting point for this survey, offering

---

* Applause, 1997.

a *locus classicus* to our bemusement. It may also produce the most sexual kind of uncanniness, although figuring out how and why this happens is no easy matter.

In *Sunrise*, where a nameless farmer and family man (George O'Brien) is having an adulterous affair with an equally nameless vacationing woman from the city (Margaret Livingston), the camera follows or accompanies him at night as he leaves his nameless wife (Janet Gaynor) and crosses a field and damp marshes to meet his lover beside a lake. But over halfway through his zigzagging trajectory, the camera suddenly slides away from him, to the left, while he exits the frame on the right. The camera then continues leftward through a dense thicket to reach the City Woman beside the lake, twirling a flower—reaching her well before the farmer does, and more directly, from a different direction. The uncanniness is the camera's unforeseeable shortcut, rushing ahead of the hero.

Here's part of what Janet Bergstrom has to say about this shot: "The shot when the husband walks into the marsh to meet the city woman in the moonlight was one of the most important for establishing the mood of the film and one of the most difficult to accomplish of all the moving shots in *Sunrise*... It begins by following the husband, then moves alongside and then ahead of him so that he walks more or less toward the camera, and then the camera moves away from him to the city woman waiting: not waiting with him, as if sharing his emotions, but waiting for him. He is no longer on-screen, and we lose a sense of where he is in the space off-screen. Exactly when and where he will re-enter the field of vision is unpredictable, to her and to us."*

---

* "Murnau's Sunrise: In-Camera Effects and Effects Specialists," chapter 18 in *Special Effects on the Screen: Faking the View from Méliès to Motion Capture*, edited by Martin Lefebvre and Marc Furstenau (Amsterdam, 2022), 357.

For Bergstrom, what's "unexpected" is the husband's arrival at the lakeside rendezvous, marking his re-entry into the shot; for me, it's not only this re-entry but also the camera's earlier departure from him and the shift in association that this necessitates. As Bergstrom implies, the camera's initial progression moves in four steps, from following the man to accompanying him to moving ahead of him to moving away from him, and if each station can be said to represent a separate viewpoint, the fourth in the series excludes us from the reckoning.

Perhaps the most confounding thing about this camera movement is the fact that even the artist we (rightly or wrongly) connect it to, F. W. Murnau, managed to misdescribe it himself, in a 1928 article, oversimplifying both its meaning and its impact:

> They say that I have a passion for "camera angles." But I do not take trick scenes from unusual positions just to get startling effects. To me the camera represents the eye of a person, through whose mind one is watching the events on the screen. It must follow characters at times into difficult places, as it crashed through the reeds and pools in *Sunrise* at the heels of the Boy, rushing to keep his tryst with the Woman of the City. It must whirl and peep and move from place to place as swiftly as thought itself, when it is necessary to exaggerate for the audience the idea or emotion that is uppermost in the mind of the character. I think the films of the future will use more and more of these "camera angles," or as I prefer to call them these "dramatic angles." They help to photograph thought.*

---

* F. W. Murnau "Films of the Future," *McCall's*, September 1928, 90.

The routine obfuscation of using "camera angles" as an abbreviation for unorthodox or unusual camera angles is compounded by an implied equivalence between camera, eye, and mind. Yet what is obfuscated the most here is whose "thought" is actually being photographed. (Whether or not Murnau's article might have been ghostwritten only complicates the issue.) Indeed, what's most confounding about this camera movement isn't that it expresses a character's thought or feeling (Is a desire a thought or a feeling?) or that it might reflect Murnau's thought or feeling (Can we call the director a character in the drama?), but that it expresses a desire that we associate with both of them yet which also appears mysteriously to function somewhat independently of either of them.

Contrary to what Murnau says, the camera movement precedes the Boy (sic) rather than follows him, and it similarly precedes us as we follow the path it has cleared for us. But when it breaks away from the Boy to express a certain impatience that seems shared by character, director, and audience, yet is also autonomous, it might be said to become slightly delirious.

Yet whose delirium is being expressed, exactly? Might it also express some of the impatience of the City Woman awaiting the Boy's arrival? And does her aggressive physical/sexual/emotional dominance over the Boy, depicted in a way that suggests a triumph of City over Country, express any aspect of Murnau's homosexuality as well, such as attraction to George O'Brien? What's confounding, in short, is the collapse of many or all of these possibilities into a fleeting moment that's really a lunge into the unknown. The "thought" or "idea" or "emotion" it captures may indeed be impatience (which is why it takes a shorter but thornier route to the adulterous rendezvous and thus deviates from an already deviant path), but whether this impatience is singular or shared remains elusive, making us both an ambiguous participant in, and a somewhat puzzled witness to, the transactions.

Winding up this slinky camera movement like a coiled spring and jamming it into the front right pocket of my jeans, I walk for several blocks to and then away from the writhing couple in the swampy marshes and towards a teeming city intersection, connected by a ride on a boat and then another ride on a trolley.

Thus desire trumps destination as the camera seems to switch from following and/or accompanying the protagonist to following the independent path of his desire. Or is it the path of the vamp's desire, pulling him towards her as if she could reel him in like a captured fish? Or is this narrative jolt really a function of both his impatient desire and hers, sharing the same compulsion with the movement of the camera? Our uncertainty becomes a shared uncanniness whereby the camera's actions speak louder than either character's words—or shared word-pictures, such as in their following scene together, when she says, "Come to the City," and a vast machine of sexual gyrations and swing-band contortions is summoned up in superimpositions, eventually giving way to her frenetic dance of illustration and evocation.

Might we conclude from Murnau's description of this sequence that he knew more about what he was doing aesthetically than he did psychologically? Perhaps. In any case, it's our uncertainty about the precise nature of Murnau's transgression that confounds us the most. The poetic links between country and tourist/city create a metaphysical space that the physicality of camera, actors, and set complicates and confuses. Much later in the film, when the reunited farmer and his wife return a night later in a rowboat across the lake from their day in the city, they pass a raft full of silhouetted, dancing Gypsies, and the rhythmic nodding of the wife's head to the music creates a visual rhyme as sexually charged and as ecstatic as the camera's earlier shortcut through the marshes. Both of these passing moments are examples of expressionist delirium in which the world itself appears to sing and dance, and certain physical movements (of camera and/or floating vessels, raft and rowboat) join the mental transports of the characters.

2.
Almost 16 minutes into Carl Dreyer's *Day of Wrath* (1943), we find a much quicker and even more devious depiction of a character walking, this time the film's heroine, the camera tracking with her as she moves across a room, our view of her periodically blocked by pillars, the camera's movement simultaneously complicated by its panning away from her as it keeps pace with her forward progress. Once again, an unsettling deviation from what we've been led to expect in terms of narrative flow, advancing and retreating at the same time.

Consequently, what we call "uncanny," or "confounding" may actually be doses of truth and reality that confound our habitual self-deceptions. If a blink equals a blank, the separate bites of reality appearing in between the blinks and blank spaces are not the same as reality plain and simple. We involuntarily con ourselves by imposing continuity over discontinuity, thereby substituting bits of ourselves for what we're defining as external reality. In short, we are the streams contextualized by what precedes this shot (the heroine encounters an older woman believed to be a witch) and what will follow it (we see and hear the older woman being tortured on a rack, stretched like taffy, much as the camera accompanying the younger woman's troubled walk stretches our perception of her to the point of replicating her pain). This time the uncanniness derives from the three-dimensional effect of the camera (i.e., us) split into two and moving in contrary directions, whereas in *Sunrise* it came from moving in the same shot from a man's point of view to a camera's independent and more impatient path.

Some necessary caveats: my lack of technical assurance about precisely what Dreyer did when he moved his camera in all his sound films makes my accounts here and elsewhere regarding *Vampyr*, *Day of Wrath*, *Ordet* and *Gertrud* amateurish guesses and approximations. The late David Bordwell in his book on Dreyer introduced me to the notion of Dreyer's camera tracking in one direction while panning in another without clarifying the effect or meaning of this maneuver, much as Noël Burch and Jorge Dana made me aware of the highly restricted use of angle/reverse angle in *Gertrud* without seriously examining its narrative or dramatic significance.* By instructive contrast, the late Tony Pipolo devoted many detailed paragraphs to this specific camera movement in an essay called "Historical Consciousness in Carl Dreyer's *Day of Wrath*"† that fully justifies both his title and Luc Moullet's contention that "Morality is a matter of tracking shots" (stated in Moullet's article on Samuel Fuller in the March 1959 issue of *Cahiers du Cinéma*, and modified by Jean-Luc Godard four months and four issues later, in a roundtable discussion of *Hiroshima mon amour*, to become the better-known "A tracking shot is a moral matter").

3. In Jacques Tourneur's *Out of the Past* (1947), the camera's independent impatience functions as a temporary and parenthetical burst of fear shared by a recently formed, impromptu couple (Robert Mitchum, Jane Greer). They both get soaked from a night storm and

---

* "Propositions" by Noël Burch and Jorge Dana, *Afterimage*, Spring 1974, 57-64.
† *Persistence of Vision*, No. 8, 1990.

a bath-towel passes between them until they're just hugging each other. She tosses the towel across the room, and it knocks over a lamp, which causes the front door to blow open and loud wind to be heard. The biggest jolt of dislocation comes in a jerky jump cut between two stages in the camera's pathway (1) out the front door and (2) (what seems much later) past the property's edges and into the darker fury of the storm itself and the cold oblivion it carries, then abruptly cutting back to Mitchum, slamming the front door, breaking the windy spell. But why in the first place does the camera choose to take such a suicidal path into the wilds? The answer, my friend, is *Written on the Wind*. Or, better yet, *Wind Across the Everglades*, but certainly not *Gone with the Wind*.

4. Orson Welles' *Mr. Arkadin/Confidential Report* (1954) comes to us in several differently edited versions, though in all or almost all of them, following a brief prologue and opening credits—including an illustrated cast list, the last member of which is Robert Arden—whom we then see, in diverse angles, while a nearby Salvation Army band is heard and seen, Van Stratten (Arden) approaching a dilapidated building in the snow, crossing its courtyard, and then, after pausing in front of an exterior staircase, hurrying up the stairs. Yet as soon as he starts climbing, the camera darts backward into what appears to be a dark tunnel—another contradictory and dialectical pair of movements like the two in *Day of Wrath*, as brief and as creepy as the track forward and pan backward in Dreyer's film. (How much is this about walking as opposed to flying? Or is it both walking *and* flying?)

One has the curious (uncanny) sensation of *being flown backward* through what feels like a tunnel that for me becomes the way one has somehow plunged (or been plunged) into a mysterious and obscure past—or more precisely, been thrown there by a sudden camera movement that pulls one away from the scene by force, like Alice falling down the rabbit hole (if such an experience could happen horizontally yet with equal force). So this is an audiovisual duet between Arden racing up the steps and the camera just as quickly fleeing from him by racing backwards, creating an implied loss of control and volition on our parts because we can't even see where we're headed as the camera yanks us there. I suspect this is why Arden's investigation into Arkadin's origins becomes a poetic inflection about how the past and future pull us in opposite directions, thus creating the existential tension that we identify and experience as the present. The fact that we don't even know who Arden is at this early stage makes the camera's retreat even more ambiguous and mysterious. And if the relation between this uncanny backward movement and our feet is more ambiguous, the fact that it seems to be propelled by Arden's feet hurrying up those stairs is what justifies its inclusion here.

5. Every shot in Alain Resnais and Alain Robbe-Grillet's *Last Year in Marienbad* (1961) is a separate departure whose source and destination are equally obscure, whereby everything becomes *in medias res,* part of an unknown, ongoing process of memory or fantasy or some dreamlike mixture of the two. And whose camera movements are we guiding or following? Are they solitary or shared imaginings? Is it one person dreaming or a power struggle over who possesses the dreams? These are the ultimate existential questions, the ones that we can never answer. Resnais said that the film could have been called *Persuasion*, but whether it's Robbe-Grillet persuading Resnais, Resnais persuading us, Giorgio Albertazzi persuading Delphine Seyrig, or maybe even all three, is never spelled out. Whoever makes these invisible or unheard agreements is kept in the shadows,

giving our imaginations more elbow room in which we can become more acquisitive. Paradoxically, although these tracking shots seem to echo rhythmically those in earlier documentary shorts of Resnais (*Night and Fog*, *All the Memory in the World*), they belong here to what we experience as an expanding fantasy.

On his website, Adrian Martin points out that the film's "opening tracking shots… five minutes' worth of them before human characters definitively appear in the image," raise many unanswerable questions.

> What are we seeing in these famous camera moves? The subjective viewpoint of someone passing through these grand mansion rooms and corridors? At some moments, it seems so. But there are also movements that only a machine (like a camera), not a human body or eye, could perform. The angle, the orientation, the flow, the rhythm, the succession, the organ music score, the montage parade – all are sweeping us into something that is at once human and not human, beyond human. We are bracingly aware of all four edges of the wide screen frame, the full extension of its changing detail – in a way we never are in life, through our eyes. Instead of our eye moving through a space, we could think of a space moving past, or through, us – or, more radically, of an altered frame as a digital-style 'resizing,' not a depth progression at all. The voice-over on the soundtrack, too, fading out and in, adds to this hide-and-seek game between the mobile frame and a potential (but *only* potential, fleeting, instantly evaporating) subjective perspective of fictional characters.*

---

* https://adrianmartinfilmcritic.com/essays/elastic_shots.html.

6. Slightly over twenty minutes into Dreyer's *Gertrud* (1964), Dreyer cuts from an almost motionless shot (the camera inching slowly to the right along with Gertrud's husband as a clock rings four times to announce the hour) to the camera already literally racing right to left along with Gertrud, Gertrud rushing across a park to meet her young about-to-be lover beside a pond—a shot that has presumably started elsewhere and elsewhen, in some netherworld of the immediate past, so that Dreyer can cut into this flow whenever he chooses, hop aboard while it's still in motion to see where it takes him. As in *Sunrise*, there's a sudden shift in narrative direction and viewpoint tied to the prospect of adultery that in this case pulls Gertrud away from her husband and towards a (much younger) piano prodigy. Let's not forget that the heroine of *Day of Wrath* also winds up cheating on her husband. Sexual transgression again leads to aesthetic transgression breaking loose.

As I've maintained elsewhere, Gertrud is a nonnarrative character trapped and struggling in a narrative world of men devoted to change.* She's capable only of mulish persistence rather than growth or development. Thus the camera movement granted to her passion is delivered to us *in medias res* and can only be partial, yet it is all the more exquisite for being abbreviated and curtailed in a passionate flash of anticipation. It's doubtful if any other camera movement discussed in this book thrills me quite as much as this one does, sculpting a carnal burst of expectation out of an actress moving through thin air beside a pond, racing towards her waiting lover. Thomas Pynchon reached for a comparable cinematic effect in *The Crying of Lot 49*: "She awoke at last to find herself getting laid; she'd come in on a sexual crescendo in progress, like a cut to a scene where the camera's already

---

* "Gertrud as Nonnarrative: The Desire for the Image," in *Placing Movies: The Practice of Film Criticism* (California, 1995), 105-116.

moving." But Dreyer's sudden nip of ecstasy is more confounding, if only because of its beauty.

7. All the characters in Béla Tarr's *Sátántangó* (1994) walk a lot, and the camera frequently moves with them, but context changes everything, so when the same moments are shown again from the viewpoints of separate characters—a palimpsest narrative strategy employed by Joseph Conrad in *Nostromo* (1904), William Faulkner in *Light in August* (1932), and László Krasznahorkai in *Sátántangó* (1985)—the effect is often uncanny regardless of whether the camera is in motion both times that a moment is depicted. In many respects, the film, split into a dozen sections, is a very close adaptation of a novel with a dozen chapters, each of which consists of a single sentence. But the novel in George Szirtes' 2012 translation is only 274 pages long whereas the film lasts 439 minutes, and each section of the movie has more than one shot and more than one camera movement. So the movement forward in a Krasznahorkai sentence is hardly the same thing as the movement forward in a Tarr shot. An important part of the difference between them is that a sentence can be both physical and metaphysical, but a camera movement can only be physical. According to Dan Gunn in his review of the novel: "What starts as a sentence happening inside one character's head ends inside a stagnation of a puddle or the terror of a cat."* Ergo, sentences can function metaphysically by moving places inaccessible to cameras, but shots can function only physically.

8. Discounting the footage borrowed from elsewhere and re-appropriated, there are basically two kinds of shots in Pedro Costa's second feature, *Casa de Lava* (1994), set mostly on a volcanic island: narrative and nonnarrative. The nonnarrative shots are generally some form

---

* *Times Literary Supplement*, June 1, 2012.

of portraiture of people and/or landscapes, commonly inserted between narrative stretches as contemplative rest stops. Sometimes Costa plays with the notion of tricking us when a supposedly motionless landscape has tiny figures walking across the bottom of the frame, one of whom happens to be the film's heroine (Inês de Medeiros as Mariana), making this a narrative shot with a nonnarrative impact. The camera movement that I have in mind is precisely the reverse of this shot of Mariana, a nonnarrative shot with a narrative impact that follows Mariana at a much closer range as she walks purposefully through a village, although we know nothing about the purpose of her walk, much less where it began and its destination. In short, we have no idea how to connect this long take with the narrative action (i.e., the story) that precedes and follows it, so we're left with a comfortable and pleasurable way of looking at Inês de Medeiros in motion with no clear narrative context.

9. From its opening shot onwards, the uncanniness of *Inside the Yellow Cocoon Shell* (2023), the Vietnamese Phạm Thiên Ân's first feature, has a lot to do with its frequent ambiguity about agency whenever the camera moves. After a stationary shot of a soccer match eventually tracks to the right to accompany a human mascot in costume walking into an adjoining café, where the camera remains stationary even longer before tracking still further to the right to frame the aftermath of a fatal traffic accident, it appears that the film's narrative is propelling the camera movement rather than Thiên (Lê Phong Vũ), the protagonist of that narrative, seen with others in the café. Only later do we discover that Thiện's sister-in-law was the fatal victim of the accident. The same disembodied effect occurs when Thiện leaves the city on a motorbike to look for his long-absent brother in the country, and the camera following his path

seems to be walking rather than motorbiking. Still later, a lengthy episode during which Thiên meets (or appears to meet) the partner and baby of his brother is revealed to be a dream via an exceptionally slow and lengthy camera movement in which Thiên appears at both ends of the shot, the camera supposedly following the path of his gaze at the beginning and then landing on his sleeping figure being woken at the end. (For comparable examples of this trick effect, cf. the "That's Entertainment" number in *The Band Wagon* [1953] and one session of the match game played by the male rivals in *Last Year in Marienbad*.)

The disembodiment effect may be Phạm Thiên Ân's most enduring gift to us—a camera that can go places without the interference of our real or virtual bodies blocking the pathways there. As with Dziga Vertov, a human eye can pretend to be a camera eye only by fakery, but once this fakery is removed, a mystical bond between spectator and scene becomes more plausible because the camera is simply a tool to bring the two together. As Godard described the process, this allows the filmmaker to become an airplane instead of an airport, a conduit for the spectator's imagination rather than some didactic endpoint, a final resting place for imagination's corpse provided by such policed institutions as Film Studies.

Postscript
Have you ever wondered what it would be like to slowly rotate while remaining absolutely still (as in *Ordet*), or to approach a woman who's walking towards you by backing away from her (as in *Day of Wrath*), or even to be suddenly caught up in the orgasmic rush of the title heroine (as in *Gertrud*), getting us to fall into the camera movement that started before the shot began, dropping into that stream without a stepping stone, as in that trick shot inside a yellow cocoon shell?

2
HOVERING OVER LANDSCAPES

A Disney cartoon map, early Vigo, Kubrick's *2001*, Lee's *25th Hour*, Ozep's *Karamazov*, Renoir and Sirk, bees, and cameras in flight

The only way you can believe that you're actually running the universe (when, in fact, no one is actually doing that) is to fly high in the sky along with Adolf and Leni as your true blue boon companions, sailing ethereally over city and countryside, ocean and land—even over the great state of Florida as represented on a life-size cartoon map at the beginning of *Dumbo* (1941), possibly the first movie I ever saw, where storks are diving down at night toward a circus, all of them carrying their precious baby bundles, eerily anticipating the spiraling attack of Hitchcock's birds on a California town. These birds are clearly dropping their diapered loads onto a map of Florida, *quelle ideé!*, a map clearly labeled as such, so that one baby bundle might land on the F, another one on the L, a third on the O, etc. Mistaking a map for reality is one of the prerequisites for ruling the roost, or at least pretending to do so like Disney and Leni.

Throughout the beginning of Jean Vigo's silent *À propos de Nice* (1930), the rule of thumb regarding motion appears to be that it should figure in every shot, either as the camera moving every which way or as the moving object or person(s) being shot by a static camera. If it's the former, it's most often from the twisty viewpoint of a plane hovering over the city. The net effect of this is to view camera movement and onscreen action as flip sides of the same coin.

More generally, flying in movies feels as natural and as effortless as it often does in dreams. The conclusions suggested by this affinity tend to be either utopian or nightmarish, depending on the church of your choice. In any case, flight in *Dumbo* equals dominating and even helping to populate the world below by transporting offspring to their parents. A world whose very existence, no matter how silly or stupid, allows children to breathe—and never mind if this should mean taking away someone else's breath, because this is a fog-eat-fog world, anyway, driven by suffocation and steamlike hisses rather than kisses. And don't forget those flying carpets in the Sabu *Thief of Bagdad* (1940) and in Walt Disney's *The Three Caballeros* (1944), carrying diverse heroes (humans in the former, cartoon birds in the latter), not to mention Mephisto's black cloak in Murnau's *Faust* and Leni Riefenstahl's almost invisible airplane in *Triumph of the Will* (1935), a shadow carrying Hitler down from the shadowless clouds to the vaulted crowds and sonorous chords of the Nuremberg rally. Flying carpets, cloaks, and shadows not only facilitate our looking down at the world. They also make camera movement the master pilot of the narrative, the driver of the shot, the *raison d'être* of movies. You can almost hear the sound of a cracking whip to celebrate the launch of this regal rule in the heavenly stratosphere, looking down at all the groveling fans, those faithful and dutiful subjects.

On the other hand, if you eliminate gravity and all sense of up and down from your movement, as in the airborne stretches of *À propos de Nice* or in outer space and much of *2001: A Space Odyssey*, what emerges is closer to gliding or swimming than to flying per se (which requires wings) and gliding or swimming in any direction. "Freefall" in these terms is a misnomer, less because of "free" than because of "fall": if you can glide any which way, even diagonally, then that can't be regarded as falling.

And "diagonally," which implies a frame and therefore an up and a down, a vertical and a horizontal, is equally improper. Movement in these conditions becomes solitary unless you're grabbing ahold of someone else, and if you do that, "free" also has to be discarded by the someone else you're grabbing. So, freedom in freefall becomes a form of solitude and/or dominance. That's why outer space tends to be scary, especially without the presumption of a camera (which imposes a frame, hence an up and down).

○ ○ ○

From my review of *25th Hour* (2002): "The classic [Spike] Lee tropes and mannerisms… include jump cuts, alternate takes of the same action (Monty and Naturelle rushing toward each other into an embrace) repeated in rapid succession, arias of ethnic abuse, and, above all, dreamy camera movements that make the characters appear to float or glide in midair, accompanied by the usual wall-to-wall music."* The dreaminess of Philip Seymour Hoffman, touched by narcissism and lust for Anna Paquin, floats across the floor at a night joint, happily burying some of the guilt he feels for being attracted to one of his high school students. The queasy uncanniness can be found in this fearful euphoria as it's being cinematically celebrated: not the same thing as adultery, but another form of social crime.

---

* https://jonathanrosenbaum.net/2023/02/feeling-the-unthinkable/.

○ ○ ○

In Fedor Ozep's *The Murderer Dimitri Karamazov* (1931), there's a feverish, sensually vibrant encirclement of an audience and singers, musicians, and dancers performing in a roomy Gypsy dive, a roving, swarming camera that keeps returning to the romantic leads before drifting away again, as if floating at random yet at the same time pulled like a magnet towards (or being sucked into) their mutual desire, and eventually winding up inside the dance of one of them, Anna Sten's Grushenka, encompassing her lap and arms as a part of that dance. The endlessly intricate, swiveling sweeps of the camera, like the buzzing of a busy bee, joining together performers and spectators, Sten's Grushenka and Fritz Kortner's Dimitri, both folded into the same musical swirls, create a robust celebration of lustful presence and community, both mysteriously enhancing one another, and even though the shot lasts barely longer than a couple of minutes, it seems to encompass a whole picaresque novel of coexistence and interactivity.

Yet it also belies a compulsiveness that won't alight on anything, a nonstop skittering across the surfaces of the world like a needle scratching a record. Arguably, its refusal or inability to stop and linger is the mark of its uncanniness. It's a shot that assures us that everything may be technically possible, but nothing is attainable or sustainable. When nothing can be settled or settled upon, the need to drift away from whatever is happening becomes part of the experience and the continuing existential dilemma: I think, even though I become clueless when a stork is carrying me to my expectant parents, who are saying as the stork approaches them, "Do drop in." And the stork actually responds to this invitation perversely and uncannily by simply dropping me. Afterthought: It's easy to see why Marilyn Monroe dreamed of playing Grushenka.

The camera never quite walks or hovers in the Gypsy dive; it drifts like a flying insect, so I can't even be sure that this is the right chapter for it. But its capacity to involve one in its textures is unmistakable. My pal (the late) Ray Durgnat, a big fan of this movie, writing for *Film Dope* in 1993: "The Karamazov film is a *tour de force* of stylistic eclecticism: 'expressionist' acting (Kortner), dynamic angles, Russian editing, marathon tracking shots. It's a real showpiece of formalism geared to psycho-lyrical ends, exactly as Eisenstein intended, except that Dostoievskian soul-torments replace Leninist collectivism to which the 'official' montage masters tuned their lyres."

The camera doesn't literally play a character in Jean Renoir's *The Crime of Monsieur Lange* (1936), but it often behaves like one, fluttering across a barroom or bedroom as if uncertain about where to go, what to look for or look at, how long to stay, and sometimes changing its fancy en route so that it darts back to its starting point. Restlessness and uncertainty are common coin in any Depression, but Renoir's version of it is so inquisitive and voracious, even celebratory, once it mutates into a socialist parable, that it often suggests the stirrings of a hyperbolically curious bee whose flight harmonizes with its elected turf. That Renoir's turf is in a constant state of becoming suggests a further instability about who we drift towards or away from, dreamers or predators—about who we are and why. As with that busy bee, our curiosity becomes part of the scenery of the courtyard community that serves as the film's narrative spine (and was tenderly evoked in Jacques Rivette's *Haut bas fragile* sixty years later) and helps to motivate the famous climactic pans leading up to the murder of the film's leading predator by its leading dreamer. The first pan proceeds upwards from the predator in the courtyard to the dreamer seen through an upstairs window, who then is followed through other windows as he moves down to the courtyard. The second pan moves horizontally 180 degrees away from the dreamer's path towards the predator, whom he kills. Without presuming to say what this very peculiar second pan "means," I think one can argue that its spatial coordinates are architectural and social as well as philosophical. Alexander Sesonske in his *Jean Renoir: The French Films 1924–1939** helpfully connects it to the film's overall "cyclical form." But one could also argue that it's another form of what Durgnat calls "stylistic eclecticism," whose bravado threatens to overwhelm its meaning.

With the reader's indulgence, I'd like to quote another film critic, Luc Moullet, expounding on Douglas Sirk's *The Tarnished Angels* in a manner that suggests a similar compulsion to move a camera for no discernible reason, tied here to Sirk's adaptation of William Faulkner's *Pylon*. Ted Fendt's 2012 translation of Moullet's 1950s review for *Cahiers du Cinéma,* excerpted here, carries no copyright, allowing me to illustrate Moullet's infamous declaration to Roland Barthes in Pesaro in 1966, "Language is theft," without any fear of legal reprisal:

> Sirk cannot adapt his personality to Faulkner's. He merely offers his not inconsiderable favorite motifs: variations on female psychology, a depiction of excess that is both critical and embellished, with this moral and metaphysical subtext that reappears from time to time in the work of the author of *Thunder on the Hill* and *The First Legion*. We don't have any right asking more of him. He accepts from the start the novel's initial facts, at least overall, without trying to give them a specific orientation. From

---

* Harvard, 1980.

this method, the result becomes necessarily Faulknerian: from its subject and structure *Pylon* is an insane novel, without a foundation. Only its aesthetic manages to give it its coherence. Considering just his out-of-the-ordinary actions—imposed mostly by Faulkner's art—Sirk, helped by the commercial tradition of adaptation that only retains the framework of a work, was obligated, so that his film would have a head and a tail, to make recourse to an overall comparable aesthetic. The difference is of degree, not of nature. One of Douglas Sirk's multiple styles is marked by the fleshing out of emptiness, exaggeration, and conspiracy—like *Summer Storm* or *Written on the Wind*, which one could say was filmed on the wind.

When one has nothing to start with, all excess, all forms of expression are good. The effects in *The Tarnished Angels* are totally gratuitous. Faulkner's technique presents, refined, this same behavior, inspiration alone dictating the tone. Who cares about verisimilitude? Attempts, variations, and disparate efforts. *The Tarnished Angels* is a faithful adaptation essentially through its use of the camera and direction of actors. The whole film is made of short, small tracking shots, generally lateral and almost invisible, the camera perpetually wandering four or five meters above the ground. Why? No reason. Just Sirk's pleasure in making his camera move. There's a very pretty shot that recalls Renoir that shows us Devlin's apartment and a surprising high angle shot when the flashback begins. There are the endless surprises with the discovery of Hudson and Malone entwined (this Dorothy is not at all worthy of Lorelei) by a masked partygoer, the unbelievable drunkenness in the apartment upstairs, the pointless glimpse of the curious old man on the first floor, the shot of Jack abandoned on the miniature, spinning airplane, while his father kills himself in a real plane. The Cinemascope compositions are extraordinarily precise and airy, without being showy. There's nothing to say about the characters. We'll never know who Devlin is, who LaVerne is, who Siggs or Roger are. And it's very good like that: the novelistic subtlety that is spoken about so much, and so often badly (cf. Antonioni, Fellini, Grémillon, Losey), is here, in the flesh, in the precise meaning of that expression. It is obtained artificially, someone will tell me: flashiness predominates, there is nothing inside. But it is because it is all surface level, that it comes just from the *mise en scène*, that it gains value. In art, there is only artifice: let's praise artifice cultivated without remorse, which thus gains a secondary sincerity, rather than artifice by itself as by others under hypocritical pretexts. The true is as false as the false; only the very false becomes true.*

This particular argument is worth citing because Sirk employs gratuitous camera movements over two decades earlier, and without any Faulknerian pretext, in the opening sequence of my favorite feature of his, the unjustly neglected *Schlußakkord* (*Final Chord*, 1936), made in Nazi Germany when he was still signing his films as Detlef Sierck, the name he was born with. Nihilism and formalism are of course international traits

---

* http://howlingwretches.blogspot.com/2012/04/moullet-on-minnelli-and-sirk.html.

and tendencies and finding them in a German soap opera about classical music or in a drunken rant delivered in Hollywoodese about a stunt pilot and his entourage seem equally appropriate (and more convincing, at least to me, than the shallow neo-Brechtian ironies of Sirk's *Imitation of Life*). Indeed, the camera movements in *Final Chord*'s opening sequence tend to be more obvious as well as more gratuitous than those in *The Tarnished Angels*—less dependent on tracks and seemingly more driven by spur-of-the-moment impulses as they dart this way and that around the action.

In both films, drunken revelry (seen in a German studio version of Central Park and environs at the beginning of *Final Chord*) provides some minimal psychological justification for the camera's activity, but the twitches and stumble-bum pans in *Final Chord* are far more blatant in following the movements of the characters than the more detached tracks of *The Tarnished Angels*, though some of this is no doubt attributable to 1930s groupthink versus 1950s loneliness and alienation. (In Hawks' *Only Angels Have Wings* and *The Thing*, which he produced, both parables about fear, these respective mindsets are eerily removed from history and then superimposed on us like alternate drafts of the same neurosis.)

One could postulate that the camera's restlessness at the beginning of *Final Chord* is as purposeful as its motionlessness a bit later when the choral climax of Beethoven's Ninth is being performed in a Berlin concert hall. There's even a moral difference in the camera's successive behaviors (recalling another famous statement by Moullet, that camera movements are a moral matter), suggesting that Sirk may have been more gainfully employed in Germany than he was in the U.S., and that he didn't want the moves of his camera to challenge or detract from Beethoven's moves.

Another movie choked with short, gratuitous camera moves, and one that's as captivated with futility as *The Tarnished Angels*, is Clint Eastwood's *Million Dollar Baby* (2004). I know that Eastwood is supposed to be a conservative and Sirk is supposed to be a Brechtian leftist, but the voluptuous defeatism embraced by both directors is strong enough to unite armchair Marxists with wizened cynics.

3
CIRCULAR REASONING IN CINEMA AS BRAINWASHING

Ordet, Vertigo, The Manchurian Candidate, Providence, and live TV dramas

A little over 11 minutes into *The Manchurian Candidate* (1962, widescreen black and white), the anonymous male narrator informs us that "The Korean War was over. Captain, now Major Bennett Marco, had been reassigned to Army Intelligence in Washington. It was, by and large, a pleasant assignment except for one thing. Night after night, the Major was plagued by the same reoccurring nightmare."

The visual accompaniment to this narration is a slow pan across a disorderly array of books on a daybed (*Ulysses* and *The Trial* rubbing shoulders with *Diseases of Horses*, among others), past a small collapsible clock that says 3:12 and an ashtray choked with cigarette butts, the camera finally landing on the troubled, sweaty, twitching features of Frank Sinatra as Marco, asleep, and then lurching forward so that his twitches in closeup become virtually the only onscreen movements.

As he softly mumbles, "Stop him" and "Stop him, Mama," there's a very slow lap dissolve to Sinatra/Marco seated, smoking a cigarette, and along with his army buddies, inside a greenhouse, listening to a middle-aged American lady in a wide-brimmed hat as she holds forth at boring length about hydrangeas while the camera slowly pans to the right to take in more listening army buddies and many more listening middle-aged or older women with hats (only one is bareheaded), except that when the 360-degree pan is complete and has started another cycle, the same listening army buddies are no longer in a greenhouse but in a Chinese operating theater backed by huge photos of Stalin and Mao. The lecturer is a Chinese Communist demonstrating for his comrades the effects of brainwashing. More precisely, the film switches to cutting between stationary camera setups; sometimes the soldiers are with the ladies and their hydrangeas and sometimes they're with their Chinese captors and hearing about their own brainwashing.

A few points about the preceding confusion:

(1) The film makes no effort to render the period setting of the early 50s in any believable or evocative way. It's hard to know whether this failure, conscious or not, is ascribable to John Frankenheimer (the director), George Axelrod (the screenwriter), and/or Richard Condon, author of the source novel, but it's a fortunate failure insofar as it matches the confusing mix of periods in many of our dreams, so that not knowing exactly where we are becomes the flip side of not knowing when or sometimes even if the events are occurring.

(2) In certain respects, Frankenheimer brought to live television drama in the '50s some of what Welles brought to live radio in the 1930s: a present-tense immediacy (especially helpful in Welles' *War of the Worlds* and Frankenheimer's *The Comedian*, both scary shows that focus on their respective media, radio and TV) that

was enhanced by quick, smooth, and fancy transitions between spaces in the same scenes. Welles' precise sense of how to move from one aural setting to another was echoed in Frankenheimer's ability to scurry across and between sets without encountering any bumps en route, creating a cubistic sense of chaos while exploring the space in deep focus. Both directors in effect made their better live productions something to be delivered like the news, hot off the press.

(3) *The Manchurian Candidate* is arguably the only Hollywood feature with an uncanny camera movement worthy of the French New Wave—or more specifically worthy of the uncanny camera movements in *Last Year at Marienbad* that similarly undermine our confidence about memories and how much they're inflected by reality or desire, the unstable terrain of our dreams. Or maybe even by an agnosticism about reality itself as this was intermittently posited by Jacques Rivette in *Paris nous appartient*, *Out 1* and *Céline et Julie vont en bateau*.

(4) Roughly 20 minutes into *The Manchurian Candidate* is another bravura sequence about competing images of reality—in this case competing camera angles of the same reality (a pastiche of Joseph McCarthy's infamous declaration about Communists lurking inside the U.S. State Department), as these are seen simultaneously "live" and on a TV screen appearing inside the "live" event. In this case, Frankenheimer frames the competing realities in a neo-cubist manner of visual juxtaposition. The outburst of Senator John Iselin (James Gregory) and its reception is seen at once from two separate vantage points, and the fact that camera movements occur periodically in one vantage point or the other only adds to the cacophony and perceived spatial chaos of the event, with Iselin's controlling wife (Angela Lansbury) hovering over the

TV image of her husband at screen left while her husband is holding forth on screen right. A psychotic temporal juxtaposition imposed by brainwashing is thus succeeded ten minutes later by the equally discomforting spatial juxtapositions imposed by TV cameras in a crowded room.

This latter effect can be traced back to Frankenheimer's nimble mise en scène five years earlier for *The Comedian* (adapted by Rod Serling from a hysterical Ernest Lehman novella) on *Playhouse 90*, partly set inside a TV studio, where the camera or cameras often come closer to the actors than if it had been a film, virtually hugging them or else bashing them together inside the claustrophobic spaces. In the show's opening shot, there is a pan first from a dense complex of TV performers and video camera, both viewed obliquely during a live broadcast, to the star of the show (Mickey Rooney as the eponymous lead, aptly named Sammy Hogarth), seen obliquely in frontal closeup on a TV monitor, and then an upward pan from there to the reaction of various crew members in closeup watching the show from a control booth, thus linking three separate viewpoints of the same event in quick succession.

For that matter, most or all of the live TV dramas presented on *Studio One* and *Playhouse 90* in the mid-1950s offer a kind of inquisitive intimacy with the actors that suggests a certain complicity with them. In *Studio One*'s original TV version of Reginald Rose's *12 Angry Men* (1954), directed by Franklin J. Schaffner — most of it set, like its cinematic successor of 1957, inside a small jury room—the camera responds to this limited space by seldom remaining still, lackadaisically drifting across the empty room even before the jurors arrive (though anticipating their arrival by moving up to the door, just before they enter in closeup) and nervously proceeding on tenterhooks thereafter as it follows one character or another, often for what appear to be arbitrary or tentative reasons. The net effect of this restlessness is a certain uncertainty about all the jurors, as if to emphasize the potential significance of every gesture in their deliberations.

This ambiguity is arguably less pronounced in the more famous, Oscar-approved 1957 film version of *12 Angry Men*, directed by Sidney Lumet, because there the juror who ultimately leads his colleagues from a guilty to a non-guilty verdict is played by Henry Fonda, leaking sincerity and virtue from every pore. Robert Cummings, less charismatic and less morally legible in the same role in the original TV version, only makes the proceedings seem more precarious and uncertain—an impression only strengthened by the novelty of live TV transmission in 1954 and our sense of impromptu human decisions lurking behind every camera move. Sometimes the nervous paths taken by the camera seem to suggest the viewpoint of a kibbitzing thirteenth juror.

I suspect that the way we watch a *Studio One* program today is different from the way we watched it (or might have watched it) seventy years ago, but it's hard to know how to extrapolate our way backwards from today into spectatorial innocence. At the age of eleven or twelve in the mid-1950s, I already associated Frankenheimer's name with quality and regarded him as a sort of auteur—*avant la lettre,* to be sure—on *Studio One*. (I was less familiar with *Playhouse 90*, which ran past my bedtime, so my discoveries of such Frankenheimer landmarks as *The Comedian* and *The Last Tycoon* would come only decades later.)

I suspect that one reason why I regarded Frankenheimer as an auteur on TV long before I recognized Samuel Fuller or Anthony Mann or Nicholas Ray as an auteur in movies was because live TV foregrounded many of the decisions made behind cameras whereas Hollywood was more adept at keeping such decisions hidden and inscrutable. The *Studio One* logo that precedes and follows the show's Westinghouse commercials has a title card flanked by two theater tickets and a pair of opera glasses resting on the same table. The implication of this quaint detail is that live TV drama hasn't yet been legitimized as a serious art form, so that props associated with a more time-tested and prestigious form of live drama might suggest that TV can offer some sort of rough equivalent. (The facts that both opera glasses and live TV dramas offer closeups is surely relevant, thus overriding the confusing fact that tickets of admission aren't required for watching anything on television.)

In order to begin to understand how the moving camera functioned on live TV dramas in the 1950s, we should first consider the creative roles played by an audience's imagination in listening to radio shows, attending live theater, and watching movies during the same period. Even though cameras had and have no role to play in radio, that medium's dexterity in shifting from one narrative space to another is part of what's being attempted in live TV drama, just as revolving stages in theater assist us in shifting from one imagined space to another.

Orson Welles' grasp of how to stimulate and then collaborate with our imaginations in radio, theater, and cinema wasn't matched by any comparable effort to expand the options of televisual narrative. Indeed, his only surviving forays in that direction, both in the 1950s — his monologues for *Orson Welles' Sketch Book* on British television and *The Fountain of Youth*, an unsold half-hour TV pilot that he made for Desilu Productions — essentially omit camera movement entirely from his technical arsenal. This is possibly because Welles' creation of a narrative centered on his physical presence as narrator/storyteller can only allow for movements projected behind him, not with him or in front of him. Significantly, *The Fountain of Youth* opens with a slide projector being loaded to offer us snapshots of the story's leading characters, and much of the story that follows comes in still photographs. Welles appears as a sort of slide lecturer to tell the story, set in the 1920s, and the theme of narcissism that comically bounces back and forth between a John Collier story about three narcissists and Welles himself as their narcissistic spokesperson becomes as static as any of the slides. (Even when the slides periodically unfreeze and briefly become live action, a sense of their being locked into a scrapbook persists.) Presumably, as in the *Sketch Book* monologues, once Welles' voice becomes the principal vehicle of narrative transport, a motionless camera is all that's needed to enlist the audience's creative collaboration. In effect, the motion in our minds serves as the motor and is our main contribution to the story.

○ ○ ○

During the final sequence of Alain Resnais' and David Mercer's *Providence* (1977), set in the luscious green backyard of novelist Clive Langham (John Gielgud), the camera slowly cranes up and then pans in a complete circle, as if to suggest, after a night full of transitions reflecting his actual or virtual drafts, that reality is every bit as ambiguous and mysterious as any novel.

○ ○ ○

Similarly, the smooth 360-degree pans opening and closing what I regard as Jafar Panahi's greatest film to date, *The Circle* (2000), whereby a prison is made to rhyme with a hospital in circumscribing the lives and fates of women in a misogynist society, are certainly worth noting and applauding.

○ ○ ○

Alexander Horwath's *Henry Fonda for President* (2024) is a three-hour essay film that mixes biography and history with social commentary, using many clips of Fonda's best-known films, Horwath's own voiceover, bits of a Fonda interview, and a few documentary shots pertaining to Fonda's family, which migrated to the U.S. in the mid-1600s, settling first in Albany, New York.

The film's first documentary shot is a lengthy pan across a couple of blocks in today's Albany, and what makes it confounding is the fact that the shot runs backwards. I asked Horwath in an email why he chose to run it backwards, and here's what he wrote back (mostly unedited, to honor the diverse twists in Horwath's thoughts):

> As for the 270-degree running-in-reverse pan in Albany that you were asking about, I tend to give an equivocal or multi-part answer to that...
>
> There is a rather simple answer which most viewers seem to find acceptable. But for [cinematographer] Michael Palm and Regina [Schlagnitweit, artistic collaborator] and me, it's only the most obvious or most rational (if also somewhat banal) one: This is the first "present-day" sequence—meaning it's the first shot in the film of material recorded on our US trips, and by shooting/running it backwards (plus: starting at a present-day site and ending on "The Oldest House in Albany" in the distance) it could signify that we are now, in the midst of our present-day moment in history, starting to also take "a tiger's leap into the past" (as [Walter] Benjamin said, even though he was referring to something else). This reverse path

into history runs alongside the "progressive," moving-forward trajectory that each film naturally has. Bluntly put: "Let's move backwards now." (During the next 3 hours, whenever we are visually in the present and mentally in the past, such "leaps" continue to occur, except that we no longer thought it necessary to have people running backwards.)

However, I believe it is never as simple as this. We spent half a day in downtown Albany, in the area of that "Oldest House" which was in the process of restoration and partly covered by an almost life-size image of what the house looked like in the past—and what it will look like once the restoration work is done. We pondered several ways of shooting that area and that house, and I felt that the widest possible pan would make the most sense in order to bring together the different layers of "material history." (We shot some closer images of the "Oldest House," too, but in the edit I decided to leave them all out because the pan worked much better as a single "sequence shot" leading us towards the church interior.) Then we thought about what would ideally be "going on" in the shot —and waited a bit, because we realized that there was a slight increase of human and car traffic, more people coming to the office. And while the man whom we follow in the shot is not me, it was—as you sensed— quite important for me to have such a "living character" occupy a central place almost all the way through that movement. If you reverse the shot now (= if you imagine the movements in their actual, running-forward reality), you'll see that we waited for a moment when a car would enter-and-leave the shot on one side and a person would enter it from the other side—and we would follow that person, in the hope that he'd make the full semi-circle around us and enter his office (the brownstone building in front of which we had placed the camera).

For all this to technically work, I first needed to be made aware of the digital camera's capacities: Michael showed this feature to me—you can decide (and you need to do it on the spot) if you want to record something in such a way that the shot can later be used "in reversed order," too, without any VFX. You can't just do it later on with any shot that you've recorded at normal speed (at least not within our budget!). So it was a conscious decision to set up (and wait for) the shot as described above. Nonetheless, it was "experimental"—I wanted to try it out and would decide much later, during editing, if it really "kept its promise."

A major reason for using the shot that way was that I wanted to avoid purism or monotony in the choice of aesthetic means and thematic explorations. In other words, while I am aware that the film belongs to a certain type of cinema and that my main influences are not very hidden, I also wanted to respect my personal weakness for the great moments of "impurity" in films. Therefore, I hoped to be able to break—at least once—certain basic (stylistic and thematic) "rules" that the work is based on. The strange Albany shot is one example of this kind of strategy, I guess.

A final aspect might be called up by what I'm narrating on the soundtrack. When we did the finetuning of image and text, I very much liked the fact that the report of the Esopus tribesmen burning down Hester Fonda's village in 1663 and taking her captive could be placed exactly where our pan in Albany "opens up" onto the central, somewhat empty park area (once a residential block, I assume) which is dominated by the massive highway/freeway construction in the background. History is always also a story of specific sites/places appearing and disappearing through human action, no matter if it's through a destructive act in the war between Native Americans and colonists in the 17th century or as a result of urban/suburban "development" in the 20th and 21st centuries…

Sorry for this VERY LONG explanation, but I wanted to relate a bit of the complicated network of feelings & experiences which, in the end, "decides" about such shots… Regina, Michael and I talked a lot about it, during the shooting as well as in the many discussions during the editing. And we reached the conclusion that the advantages of the shot (some more obvious than others) are much stronger than its potential disadvantages (that it might be viewed as a somewhat childish way of entering history).

4
F. W. MURNAU AND THE POETICS OF DELIRIUM

Among many other things, F. W. Murnau (1888–1931) deserves to be called the silent cinema's expressionist poet of delirium, with a talent for finding diverse technical solutions to the challenges of capturing and illustrating various delirious states of mind.

Most of his early work hasn't survived, and the earliest manifestations of his talent for poeticizing subjectivity that I'm familiar with come not in *Nosferatu* (1922), his eleventh feature—a great horror film, but one whose natural locations resist the sort of expressionist inflections that can be created in studios—but in *Phantom*, his twelfth (and the last of his four features to be released in 1922).

Despite its title, *Phantom* isn't a horror film. It's a melodrama charged with German Romantic griefs and swoony transports, adapted by Thea von Harbou from a novel by Nobel laureate Gerhart Hauptmann that wasn't published until 1923. Like *Metropolis*, which von Harbou would later co-script, it has an aggressive female doppelganger heroine (the "good" Veronika and the "bad" Mellitta, both played by Lya de Putti) and a very passive and immature hero, Lorenz (Alfred Abel).

The complex sequence with these two that I wish to discuss lasts only two minutes and begins a little after 93 minutes into the film. I can't pretend to do justice here to its fifteen shots, briefly described below, but should note that Janet Bergstrom does an excellent job of showing how the twelfth shot was technically realized in her video *Invitation to Phantom* that's included on the DVD of the "authorized restored version" released by Flicker Alley, an edition that also includes drawings and helpful notes by art director Hermann Warm.

> 1. Intertitle: "The topsy-turvy day…"
> 2. Lorenz and Mellitta are shown from above, racing right-to-left down a semicircular slice of a stairway. Cut to
> 3. Mellitta and Lorenz enter a fancy restaurant, moving left-to-right into the frame, with much affectionate gesticulation on Mellitta's part, before two waiters simultaneously remove each of their overcoats. Cut to
> 4. The two of them dancing on the crowded dance floor, the camera following them as they glide past other dancers, moving right-to-left. Cut to
> 5. A closeup of Lorenz, who seems out of sorts. Cut to
> 6. Mellitta and Lorenz seated in a carriage while the city street behind them recedes in a very blatant, phony-looking rear-projection. Fadeout.
> 7. Fade into their shopping spree (dresses, hats, and flowers in 7, 8, and 9), before returning to (10) the same camera setup of them seated in a "moving" carriage, this time with packages in their laps. Cut to

11. Mellitta and Lorenz at a restaurant table in the same establishment—the former eating and drinking, the latter clearly out of sorts before she gestures for him to drink up and he promptly pours and gulps down two glasses of wine as we cut to

12. A closeup of Lorenz looking lost and dizzy and even more out of sorts before we cut to

13. A shot over their table that steadily rises higher and higher until we arrive at

14. (I know this sounds crazy, but) three parallel circular tracks around which a motorcyclist is speedily racing, left-to-right and right-to-left, until we cut to

15. A tilted point-of-view shot moving (or maybe I should say lurching) across the dance floor in a right-to-left 360-degree circle before we cut to…

There's a bit more dancing and lurching, and all the counter-movements orchestrated by Murnau—right-to-left always followed by left-to-right, and vice versa, whether it's the camera or the characters moving or both, not to mention the fake movement of obvious rear-projection or the climactic vertical movement upward and backward into uncharted territory (like that reverse horizontal plunge at the beginning of *Mr. Arkadin*), arriving at a motorcyclist defying gravity by moving in horizontal circles—produce an embodiment of sheer topsy-turvy dizziness, losing one's balance and one's bearings, poetically and musically woven into a narrative. One kind of delirium delivered cinematically.

Another kind, connected more directly to drunkenness, is found two years later, in *Der letzte Mann* (*The Last Laugh*, 1924). But even though Murnau is happy to keep his camera motionless whenever he wants to record

Emil Jannings' hammy performance, he depends on diverse forms of camera movement (including an impression of walls rotating around the character to convey his dizziness), as well as blurry focus to capture the character's subjective states just before and during a drunken delirium that isn't the same thing as hysteria, but they do seem to belong together and coexist in some of Jacques Rivette's best films, stretching from *Paris nous appartient* and *L'amour fou* to *Out 1* and *Céline et Julie vont en bateau.*

5
PERPETUAL MOTION IN ALTMAN'S *THE LONG GOODBYE*

As I had occasion to write a half-century ago: "In Michael Tarantino's article 'Movement as Metaphor' [which originally appeared in the same issue of *Sight and Sound*], a persuasive case is made through concrete evidence that the nearly constant and often gratuitous movement of the camera in *The Long Goodbye* affects both our relationship to the film and [detective Philip] Marlowe's relationship to the world around him."* More precisely, as I presently experience it, the moral placements of both Marlowe and the film's viewers are cast adrift in a kind of affectless stupor, a pot-induced haze of perpetual bemusement combining curiosity and bafflement. The camera movements that perform this doomsday dance include tracks, pans, and zooms —anything, in short, that keeps us in perpetual motion, often for no particular expository reason in relation to the complicated gumshoe plot. What mainly registers from this movement is a kind of permanent restlessness that is most often experienced as a neurotic tic more than a moral or intellectual position.

---

* "Improvisations and Interactions in Altmanville," *Sight and Sound*, Spring 1974

Tarantino's detailed analysis, focusing on seven pivotal scenes, eventually concludes that a sort of dialectical pattern of movements canceling one another out prepares us for the shock of the final scene, when Marlowe shoots his best friend and dances away to the strains of "Hooray for Hollywood" heard on the soundtrack. Michael Tarantino, oddly anticipating the debut of Quentin Tarantino, translates this anomaly into the following conclusion: "Each camera movement works in two simultaneous modes—the immediate and the ultimate. Hollywood is dead! Long live Hollywood!"

Robert Altman noted that the movie's central premise was to turn Marlowe into a version of Rip van Winkle, waking up (as he does in the opening shot) into a world where the medieval sense of morality that had once guided him (as a veritable knight in shiny armor, at least according to Raymond Chandler's glittering prose) in a world where such moral certainty had vanished. But as often would happen with Altman, his stylistic assurance was accompanied by a certain intellectual confusion, so that for him the "ultimate" decision of Marlowe to kill his best friend in Leigh Brackett's screenplay was, for him—as he explained in a filmed interview*—essential to his agreement to direct that script. For me, however, Marlowe committing murder at the end of the picture rings false, in part because it replaces his and our moral uncertainty with the ersatz complacency of a tit-for-tat movie revenge plot. We basically take this ending as a dandy's pose, a piece of familiar genre baggage, and a default gesture rather than an existential decision or a moral position. Like Altman's use of closeups of the American flag as an inflated piece of rhetoric in the final sequence *of Nashville* (which is conveniently and perhaps desperately made to stand for both everything

---

* https://www.youtube.com/watch?v=uvWDhoQ9oDc.

and nothing), it arguably offers itself as a reliable standby more than as a logically arrived-at conclusion.

Much as Altman's *The Player* (1992) would later condemn Hollywood as phony and hollow while gleefully inviting its audience to recognize almost as many stars in guest appearances as one could find on Oscar night, *The Long Goodbye* ultimately and fatally plays both ends against the middle. But before it does so, it creates a nightmarish vision of greater Los Angeles in which constant camera movement has the paradoxical effect of taking us both everywhere and nowhere, comprising a nervous twitch more than a principled desire to get to the bottom of things—which becomes a pointless aspiration once there is no bottom.

By contrast, the compulsive camera movements in Fellini's *8½* (1963) are a principled way of asserting that life is movement and movement is celebration, so that going everywhere is not quite the same thing as going nowhere. The celebratory circle of people marching around Guido (Marcello Mastroianni) at the end of the film, like planets rotating around a sun or performers dutifully "making the rounds" of a circus ring, offers both an end to Fellini's film and a beginning to Guido's. This poetic choreography of encirclement offers a psychological meaning to both films that bears some resemblance to a moral, albeit a moral predicated on an amoral entitlement that comes with power.

The camera in Kira Muratova's *Melody of a Street Organ* (*Melodiya dlya sharmanki*, 2009) is even more restless as it follows two hungry and homeless siblings through Christmas street crowds, looking for their long-lost father, but here the multiplicity of camera moves above, below, after, before, and/or with the wandering children has no psychological meaning apart from the frustrations of an endless quest. A work of social protest about the callousness of grown-ups, mainly illustrated in Felliniesque cartoons, it takes on cosmic implications when its progress is rendered through overhead cranes and is more prosaic when it sticks to following the kids at street level, but it rarely shows us anything about the protagonists that the mainly indifferent adults don't see. Muratova's characteristic embrace of society's rejects doesn't have room for the sort of mental spaces evoked by Fellini's camera moves. The surfaces of a neorealistic social landscape predominate even in stagey urban sets. To put things more simply, camera movements in *8½* are expressive pathways into a hero's inner states; in *Melody for a Street Organ*, they're scattered impulses stuck in exteriors, like a fly repeatedly colliding into a screen door.

6
EARLY OZU: CAMERA MOVEMENT AS INSPECTION

> NOTEBOOK: What are your personal favorite Ozu films? Are there any that have special meaning for you?
> HASUMI: [*In Japanese*] My favorite is *That Night's Wife* [1930].
> NOTEBOOK: Can I ask why?
> HASUMI: [*In English*] Because the film is very Hollywoodian.
>
> > "This Second Is Eternal: Shiguéhiko Hasumi on *Directed by Yasujirō Ozu*" by K. F. Watanabe, posted on MUBI Notebook.*

Hasumi has also stated more than once that his liking for Japanese cinema stems in part from its resemblance to Hollywood by being a form of studio cinema. To which I should add that the first Ozu feature I ever became enthusiastic about in print, after first seeing it in 1972 at

---

*https://mubi.com/en/notebook/posts/this-second-is-eternal-shiguehiko-hasumi-on-directed-by-yasujiro-ozu, April 15, 2024.

the Paris Cinémathèque's first Ozu retrospective, was indeed *That Night's Wife*, or *Wife for a Night*, as it was then known to me. Here's what I wrote about it for the Summer 1972 issue of *Film Comment*:

> The décor itself is an extraordinary assemblage suggesting both a studio stockroom and a Sternbergian junkpile: posters of Hollywood films (*Broadway Scandals*) and foreign countries (India), a full clothesline, an English motto scrawled in chalk ("Two's company, three's a crowd"), scattered snapshots and clogged ashtrays comprise only a fraction of the terrain. Recalling the travel posters on the claustrophobic stairway in Nicholas Ray's *Bigger Than Life*, one quickly realizes that Ozu is using camera movements to express the same sort of relationships that Ray can show in Cinemascope with a motionless camera. And implausible as the connection might seem, the vastly different sensibilities of Ozu and Ray are linked by a common obsession: the importance of the horizontal line. (This connection may appear somewhat more plausible if we consider Ray's statement that his "appreciation for the horizontal line" derives from his studies with Frank Lloyd Wright, and then acknowledge the almost exclusive influence of Japanese art and architecture on Wright's architecture.)
>
> If I compare Ozu to an Occidental director […], this is not to overlook the fact that in Japan he is commonly considered the "most Japanese" of directors. But since Ozu is firmly labeled esoteric in the West, an examination of a few points of convergence with European and American directors may help to demonstrate that his social, aesthetic, and cultural orien-

tations are not as remote to us as many have assumed. Indeed, rather than insist that Ozu can only be understood from a Japanese viewpoint, it is much more rewarding to assume that one's own cultural biases are both necessary and adequate. In this context, it is worth noting that, according to Donald Richie, Ozu's favorite film was *Citizen Kane*, and that he spoke with enthusiasm about Thomas Ince, Rex Ingram, Chaplin, and Ford; and the American posters in *Wife for a Night* are only a foretaste of the increasingly Americanized landscapes of Ozu's later films, from various shots of Tokyo's Time-Life building in the late 40s to the pastel-plastic colors and surfaces of *Equinox Flower* (1959).

For all the apparent stylistic differences between *Wife for a Night* and Ozu's postwar films, they are clearly the work of the same man. The celebrated scene-setting shots in the later films, compressing a locale and milieu into a single emblematic image, are prefigured by the startling aptness of certain closeups that distill and abstract complex strains in the plot, such as a beautiful image of the robber's hand fluttering nervously against the glass pane of a phone booth as he tries to place a call. And one could say that the stationary medium shots of the later period, which snugly frame the characters in their home environments, are themselves distillations of the horizontal linkage implied by the camera movements in *Wife for a Night*.

This early and awkward appreciation was of course over a decade before I read the first edition of Shiguéhiko Hasumi's book about Ozu in French translation, and over a half-century before the publication of the English translation of the book's second edition, which occasioned the Watanabe interview cited above. It may or may not have played a role in Hasumi inviting me to join him on an Ozu panel in Tokyo in 1998 (my text for this panel, entitled "Is Ozu Slow?", can be found on my website, jonathanrosenbaum.net). But the tendency in Japan and North America alike to privilege Ozu's sound pictures (which tend to have less awkward and obscure English titles) and their relative lack of camera movements is what has inspired me to offer the present chapter, predicated on the distinctive camera movements of both *Wife* and my favorite Ozu feature today, the equally silent *I Was Born, But...* (1932), which has a no less peculiar English title of its own.

Why, you may be asking, am I devoting a chapter to Ozu's camera movements rather than those of Kenji Mizoguchi? Basically, because it's the formal logic of Ozu's camera movements performing a kind of formal inspection that interests me here. (The lengthy camera movement in Mizoguchi's *The Story of the Last Chrysanthemums* [1939] that follows the noble hero and servant heroine from below the embankment is memorable and weird, but I don't know what else I could say about it.)

The best example of Ozu's formal inspection occurs early in *I Was Born, But...*, in a gag that may be the most self-referential moment to be found in Ozu's surviving work: comparing the regimented conformity in the little boys' school with the regimentation and conformity in their father's office, Ozu shows the boys marching briskly past the camera in their schoolyard while the camera is beginning to track rapidly in the reverse direction. Then there is a cut to another rapid track in the father's office, moving at the same speed past workers at a row of desks, some of them seated and some standing. Each worker yawns as if on cue just as the camera moves past him, except for one worker—until the camera moves back, stops, and waits for him to yawn as well; as soon as he does so, the camera resumes the same rapid movement past other workers, all of whom yawn again on cue.

It's a comic statement about authority—Ozu's authority (and his control) over his actors and other materials, and society's authority over its institutions—as well as the standardization/conformity arising from both Ozu's and society's forms of control. And even though there's hardly any comedy in *Wife for a Night* (although its title seems to belong to a comedy), there's a similar sense of "taking inspection" when the camera tracks past a line of policemen in the film's prologue, and a simple sense of authority once a pistol becomes pivotal in ordering the mise en scène inside the cluttered flat, as if the pistol was serving as a surrogate for the camera in establishing control and authority over a given space.

In 1988, on the Tokyo University campus, where Hasumi was then serving his four-year term as elected president, was a fascinating exhibition including, among much else, some of Ozu's monomaniacal notebooks in which he neatly and meticulously recorded both the precise length of each shot (in minutes and seconds) in a particular feature of his as he predicted, planned, and/or ordered it, and the precise length of the shot eventually achieved. This perfectly illustrates Ozu's quiet obsessiveness at full tilt—formal inspection ultimately giving way to a chart-like form of self-judgment spelled out in numbers, yielding a tally sheet.

7
ALAIN RESNAIS AND THE ART OF DISAVOWAL: THE DISCREET CHARM OF THE TRACKING SHOT

Known for both his shyness and his identity as a self-styled Surrealist, Alain Resnais (1922–2014) was also the most daring and risk-taking figure of the French New Wave, surpassing even Godard and Rivette in his capacity to reinvent himself with every fresh project. Yet he also sought to conceal himself far more than any of his colleagues, disavowing his creative impulses and his taste for experiment so thoroughly that they remained obscure to most of his public, who tended to misread his timidity as coldness. His increasing reluctance to give interviews gave him even more opportunities to use his shyness as a shield.

For those who associate the *nouvelle vague* with film critics writing for *Cahiers du Cinéma*, Resnais was clearly an outlier. He wasn't a critic at all, though as a teenage movie buff during the German Occupation, he introduced André Bazin, only four years older, to silent cinema in general and German Expressionist cinema in particular. For that matter, he shared with Godard and Rivette a talent for exposing his critical tastes in his own filmmaking so that, for example, his personal appreciations of Hollywood romantic melodramas and MGM musicals are fully apparent in the echoes of *Gilda's* editing in *Last Year at Marienbad* and the evocations of *Gigi's* plushness in *Not on the Lips*, respectively.

Hiding behind his collaborators (especially his screenwriters) didn't prevent him from making films as personal and even sometimes as autobiographical as his more outspoken colleagues. Resnais, master of the mysterious camera movement and its poetic rhetoric, was perhaps the only Surrealist to make camera movements serve Surrealist ends almost systematically, across most of his professional career, which began with *Van Gogh* (1949), a short that often consists of camera movements traversing various canvases. This imposition of itineraries on how to look at particular paintings has often struck me as meddlesome and unhelpful, but obviously many people disagree with me, because the film won Resnais his only Oscar, and he applied the same scanning principle to his *Gauguin* (1950).

It could be argued that certain auteur-like traits recur in Resnais' work, even when he appears to be avoiding or disowning them. Sometimes this is a matter of his camera movements directly or indirectly commenting on one another. Thus the exterior lateral tracking shots around abandoned concentration camps in *Night and Fog* (1955) are recalled in the interior tracking shots through the Bibliothèque Nationale in *All the Memory in the World* (1956), inspiring the reflection made by some commentators (and by Resnais himself) that the books in these shots are treated like prisoners.

Furthermore, the use of camera movements associated with recalling or imagining or brooding over unseen past incidents recurs in Resnais' first two fiction features,

Hiroshima mon amour (1959) and *Last Year at Marienbad* (1961), both of which foster a great deal of ambiguity about what separates documentary from fiction and mental reality from objective physical reality. Both features are structured around extended dialogues between a man and woman, and the roles played by moving cameras in establishing both a sense of objective reality and a sense of subjective reality are both complex and ambiguous. A "dialogue" between Resnais and Marguerite Duras during the making of *Hiroshima mon amour* consisted of Resnais traveling to the title city and scouting or filming locations while corresponding with Duras back in France. (Portions of Resnais' side of the correspondence were later included on DVDs and Blu-rays of the film.) To oversimplify the roles played by camera movement and editing in establishing objective and subjective aspects of reality, it might be said that a pan across a twitching hand in *Hiroshima* serves as a portal into a Proustian seizure by which the past forcibly overtakes the present, whereas the tracking shots in *Marienbad* in and around diverse hotel settings simultaneously evoke memory and imagination (although whose remains unverified), non-fiction and fiction—a sustained and unresolvable ambiguity about whose reality or unreality is being examined, as if the documentary tracks of *Night and Fog* and *All the Memory of the World* were being transferred *in toto* to a fantasy universe where elegance reigns but one person's imagination can easily be mistaken for another's within that luxury. It's an infant's kind of drift, viewed as if from a baby carriage as it wheels or dollies its way through gaping and frozen hotel interiors.

The two film masterpieces of Ebrahim Golestan, *Brick and Mirror* (1963) and *The Crown Jewels of Iran* (1965), both attack the country's ruling class and rely on camera movement to express part of their anger and despair about class inequities. Even though the former, a feature, seems to reflect the influence of Antonioni as environmental commenter, the influence of Resnais on the latter, a short film, is even more pronounced and pertinent. For me, the climactic shot in *Brick and Mirror,* following a documentary sequence devoted to homeless children in a hospital, is a slow track away from the stricken heroine in a corridor after having seen and interacted with these kids, confounding us with the seeming boundless reaches of the corridor where she's standing—which we're encouraged to equate, emotionally if not literally, with the enormity of what she's just seen: the fact that we can't bear for the camera to back away from her any further represents our inability to cope with the size of the problem. That Golestan essentially belonged to the same ruling class that he was indicting only adds to the shot's abstraction as it moves with the camera from physical reality to metaphysical impact. (Earlier in the film, jump cuts following the taxi-driver hero's path up a steep embankment express some of the same helplessness in coping with a problem in all its vastness—an effect that in this case evokes Orson Welles' film of *The Trial*.)

Two early short films of Resnais and three early Resnais features can be regarded as a single theme-and-variations work ruminating about what camera movement can or might entail, and this investigation recurs in many of Resnais' subsequent films. In *Muriel* (1963), his third feature, a film without a flashback (although much of the dialogue concerns ruminations about a troubled past), the only tracking occurs in the final shot, when a formerly unseen character enters and explores an otherwise empty flat that has formerly served as the film's main location. I've already described in this book a 360-degree camera movement near the end of *Providence* (1976), around a leafy backyard that can be regarded as a celebration of objective reality in broad daylight after a night filled with the drunken imaginings of an elderly novelist, or maybe as just another form of dreaming. There's also an epic crane shot moving across much of a house's exterior in *Wild Grass* (2009) that might be said to serve a somewhat similar function. In fact, most of Resnais' filmography can be viewed as a developing dialogue between many camera movements, each of which remembers or revises a previous camera movement that it responds to. *Marienbad* includes as many of these responses as it can find room for, most of which are questions rather than answers, helping to explain why so many questioning mirrors recur in the camera's inquisitive pathways.

All of these films seem to hover over the question of how one might reconcile the past with the present. (The books in the Bibliothèque Nationale in *All the Memory of the World* might be said to represent recordings of the past as well as "prisoners," although this is the only film among these five that isn't directly concerned with trauma arising from a repressed or suppressed memory.)

I believe we can postulate throughout Resnais' filmography a kind of dialectical collaboration between legato camera movements and staccato cuts that create his most expressive moments: the cut to an underwater swimmer rising to the water's surface in *Statues Also Die* (the short documentary and polemic about African sculpture he made with Chris Marker that arguably establishes the greatness of both filmmakers at the onset of their oeuvres) is as meaningful a moment as the twitching hand of the sleeping Japanese hero in *Hiroshima mon amour*.

To my taste, the most striking instance in Resnais' work of one camera movement commenting on or "replying" to another occurs in his late masterpiece *Mélo* (1986), and because I've already written about this film in some detail elsewhere,* I hope I can be forgiven for quoting from that essay here. The first of Resnais' films to

---

* "Alain Resnais and *Mélo*," *The Chicago Reader*, April 15, 1988 and https://jonathanrosenbaum.net/2024/01/alain-resnais-and-melo.

qualify as an adaptation of a pre-existing work (a play by Henri Bernstein, written and set during the late 1920s), it focuses on a married couple and their best friend:

> All three of these characters are musicians, and many of the film's most intense passages occur when they are either performing music (usually together) or recollecting earlier performances. Resnais has consciously extended this principle by "scoring" and "conducting" the dialogue as if it were itself music. The two longest and most mesmerizing cadenzas in the film are monologues contained in single shots, accompanied by nearly continuous camera movement and subtle lighting changes.
>
> In the first, near the beginning, Marcel Blanc (André Dussollier) recounts to his old music-conservatory chum Pierre Belcroix (Pierre Arditi) and Pierre's wife Romaine (Sabine Azema) a story that seeks to explain why years ago he gave up hoping for a love of total trust. On tour in Havana with his mistress Hélène, he played Bach's *Third Violin Sonata* at a concert, addressing it and his emotions directly to her in the front row—only to discover her exchanging glances with a stranger several seats away, a gesture that she lied about later when he questioned her about it.
>
> In the second cadenza, near the end, a few years after the suicide of Romaine—who began a brief, secret affair with Marcel the day after he delivered the above-mentioned monologue—her husband and Marcel's friend, Pierre, recites to Marcel by heart the letter that she wrote to him before drowning herself in the Seine.

> The musicality of both of these monologues is intensified by very slow camera movements—beginning in both cases with Pierre and ending on Marcel—and by changes in lighting that occur along the way, changes that have no realistic causes but serve dramatic ends. The first camera movement drifts from left to right behind Pierre and Romaine—who (like the camera) are facing Marcel at the other end of a table—before moving into a closeup of Marcel. The successive configurations on the screen during this remarkable lengthy take are as follows: Marcel-Pierre-Romaine; Pierre-Marcel-Romaine; Romaine-Marcel; and Marcel alone. This series is a "musical" prefiguration, as it were, of the drama as a whole as seen from Marcel's viewpoint; the story begins with Marcel set apart from the married couple, continues with Marcel intervening between them, and then focuses on Romaine and Marcel together, before concluding with Marcel alone. In the second cadenza, while Romaine's suicide letter is being recited by Pierre, the camera traverses the increasingly dark stretch of empty space between Pierre and Marcel, until it finally arrives at Marcel's tear-stained face. The darkness "stands in" for the missing Romaine.

Although I agree with most of this account several decades later, I regret my too-easy acceptance of the classbound bubble in which all the characters reside and the emotional repression that keeps their shared bubble intact.

In passing, the "subtle lighting changes" alluded to above, employed in both *L'amour à mort* (1984) and *Mélo*, were inspired by the dramatic changes made in lighting without realistic justifications that Resnais found in comic strips by Milton Caniff, best known for his *Terry and the Pirates*. I came upon this surprising fact in François Thomas' *Trente Ans avec Alain Resnais: Entretiens*,* and it seems important to mention it here because it exemplifies Resnais' critical perceptions as a fan of popular culture (including comic strips and stage musicals as well as movies) rather than as an intellectual or a theorist, contrary to the way he's commonly and mistakenly regarded in Anglo-American circles. Like his unorthodox camera movements, Resnais' various experiments may register like avant-garde gestures, but they most often seem to derive from a mainstream taste.

Notable exceptions: Hans Werner Henze's modernist scores for *Muriel (1963)* and *Love Unto Death (1984)*. The latter is only heard in shots kept separate from the story. The beauty and terror of an indeterminate space intervening every time a patch of music is heard shifts in clarity and presence, making it even more indeterminate. Sometimes it's just darkness, a sea of empty black, and sometimes it's different shades and hues of darkness, filled with drifting clumps of some sort of cosmic dust. A key facet of this minimal image of drifting dust, no matter what version of it appears, is that you can't tell (at least I can't) whether the camera is moving or not. There's plenty of movement, visible and even tactile, but whose?

The same spatial ambiguity and sense of abstraction are felt throughout Golestan's *The Crown Jewels of Iran*, implying a cosmic divide between classes that can only be described but not breached, much like the divide between life and death represented allegorically and poetically in *Love Unto Death*. Formally, the film alternates between motion and stasis but also complicates our sense of each register through hyperbolic presentations. The crown

---

* Les Impressions Nouvelles, 2022.

jewels are often shown in perpetual motion inside an abstract space—seemingly rotating and becoming larger or smaller without any anchoring context that would allow us to determine whether it's the jewels or the camera or both that are in motion. Golestan's contrasting static shots of landscapes and workers suggest a cosmic divide between royal jewels and Iranians that resembles Resnais' abstract division of life and death into separate shots and sound environments—a division made palpable by the anger of Golestan's voiceover (which led to the suppression of this state-supported documentary, as happened earlier with the final reel of Resnais' and Marker's *Statues Also Die*, which attacks French racism and imperialism).

Returning to *Love Unto Death*, the Henze music assumes full authority to deliver a statement of its own that suggests a sort of Greek chorus to the action (or else a disconnected set of unrelated interludes, which is also possible) about an archeologist (Pierre Arditi) who dies and comes back to life, as witnessed by his botanist lover (Sabine Azema), in the film's opening sequence, before the two of them spend the remainder of the film struggling with all the consequences. It isn't so much a class bias as the presence of a certain gloss that only smoothly moving cameras can bring, i.e., the same sort of class bias that was already an essential part of the MGM message. And as a somewhat rich kid myself who grew up under the spell of MGM's patriarchal images and pretensions, I have to admit that my own appreciations of Resnais, Welles, Golestan, Ophüls, and Godard, such as my above celebrations of *Mélo*'s multiple tenses, are to some extent endorsements and applications of luxury, even when they carry troubled subtexts, as they often do in *Sunrise*, *Le plaisir*, *Marienbad*, *Weekend*, *Stavisky*, *Mélo*, both Golestan films and Welles' first two features. So rather than search the works of Souleymane Cissé, Ousmane

Sembène and Abbas Kiarostami for confounding camera movements out of some PC sense of guilty-liberal duty rather than any unprompted sense of discovery, I would prefer to explore the ideological biases that govern some of my aesthetic preferences regarding Resnais & Company.

The deepest emotions in *Mélo* are repressed and sublimated into musical performance and/or camera movements, two forms of flow that are periodically allowed to stand for one another. They can express what the characters' words cannot. *L'Amour à mort* and *Mélo* are tied in both cases to the maximal status of music, causing the narrative flow to stop and wait for it whenever it's heard. The Sondheim score for *Stavisky*, tied at one point to a Lubitischian crane creeping around a hotel's exterior while Charles Boyer enters it more properly from the front, accompanies a duet of their right-to-left trajectories that is interrupted by a savage cut to a closeup of Stavisky's wife Arlette (Anny Duperey) being startled by Boyer's knock at her door, as if she's just been rudely awakened from a dream. This is a lyrical camera movement with a sting in its tail. When I interviewed Resnais on set during the film's production, he told me he wanted the film to be like a piece of sweet pastry with a bitter almond hidden inside it. That cut to Duperey's face in *Stavisky* may be one of the creepiest shots in any Resnais film, and it's over so quickly that it feels like a mirage of impending doom predicting the characters' futures.

Jean-Luc Godard's *Weekend* (1967)—another attack on the ruling class from a member of that class (whose online exchanges with Golestan provide the substance of Mitra Farahani's 2022 film *See You Friday, Robinson*)—also uses camera movement to express enormity, most memorably in a tracking shot past an endless traffic jam, but also in the double-encirclement of a rural courtyard during the on-site performance of a Mozart piano sonata by screenwriter Paul Gégauff. And of course, some of the troubled camera movements of Orson Welles, another spoiled rich kid and guilty liberal, are the apotheosis of his dark appreciations of luxury, especially in his first two features.

8
FOUR DYNAMIC METAPHYSICAL MOVEMENTS

1

In Orson Welles' *Citizen Kane* (1941)—shortly after the beginning of its first flashback, 19 minutes into the film—the camera pulls back from a boy sledding down a hill in the snow, proceeding through an open window in a cottage where the boy's mother (Agnes Moorehead), standing next to his prospective guardian (George Coulouris), is calling out to him. The camera continues to move backwards into the room, taking in the boy's father (Harry Shannon) and a table where a legal document is about to be signed.

Unlike the quicker backward camera movement near the beginning of *Mr. Arkadin*, cited in the first chapter, which evokes a plunge into the past, this one implicitly comments on the boy's future by contradicting his apparent freedom and sealing his fate with his mother's signature. Paradoxically, the wider the visual field becomes, the narrower the prospects for the future. So the camera movement makes it seem preordained.

2.

In Carl Dreyer's *Ordet* (1955), Johannes (Preben Lerdorff Rye), a young man who's seemingly mad enough to think he's Jesus, is seated at screen center while his niece, a child named Maren (Ann Elisabeth Rud), approaches him from behind, and sits beside him while her mother, Inger, lies dying offscreen only a room away, having already just lost her newborn baby. Cut to a closer shot of the two characters, adult and child, in profile. From a different angle, the camera appears to move very slowly around them in almost a full circle while the scenery in the room appears to glide correspondingly. Yet the camera never frames these characters from behind at any point in its nearly 360-degree rotation. They remain positioned either frontally or in profile, with Maren lit more brightly than Johannes throughout the sequence.

So apparently it isn't so much the camera as a part of the set that's moving. Yet the fact that we don't really know what we're watching is part of the scene's meaning and significance.

Like *The Passion of Joan of Arc*, *Vampyr*, *Day of Wrath* and *Gertrud*, *Ordet* is a film about both belief and challenges to belief, conviction as well as challenges to conviction—the focus of the conversation we hear between Johannes and Maren. By keeping us spellbound with this dialogue, Dreyer slyly challenges our belief in the veracity of a scene that is actually physically impossible, creating a miracle with his own form of movie magic in order to prepare us for another kind of miracle in the film's final sequence. Implicitly, he's telling us that if we can accept this miracle without realizing that we are doing so, surely we can accept the miracle of Inger's resurrection that will follow soon afterwards.

3.

In Michael Snow's *Wavelength* (1967), a camera appears to move across the length of an 80-foot urban loft through a series of periodic jerks and over occasional shot changes, proceeding towards four double windows, three intervening sections of wall space, a desk, radiator and chairs, finally focusing on a photograph of sea waves posted on the wall. In the middle of this apparent journey, a man (Hollis Frampton) enters the frame and drops dead, and the zoom continues past him. Later, a woman (Amy Taubin) enters the frame and makes a phone call describing her discovery of the man's dead body.

Even though Snow is moving his camera's zoom and not moving his location, it quickly becomes apparent that the film's forward motion, its "narrative," can't be equated with its zoom, because the constant transformation of the image involves many other changes. As Annette Michelson describes these changes in her 1971 essay "Toward Snow," they include "the occurrence, throughout the film, of color flashes in a range of extraordinary intensity, of sudden changes in the field from positive to negative, of superimposition of fixed images over the progressive zoom, itself by no means absolutely steady, but proceeding with a slight, optimal stammer," to which she adds, in the following sentence, "the evidence of splice marks" and "the use of varying film stocks."* In short, a lot more than any so-called camera movement, which might in any case be regarded as a misnomer inasmuch as it's only a camera's zoom lens that's in motion.

We're a bit like those pre-Galileo simpletons who think that the sun must be revolving around the earth because we're always at the center of God's attention and the show is ultimately about us (and we are what's histor-

---

* Annette Michelson, "Toward Snow," in *On the Eve of the Future* (MIT, 2017), 167; 170.

ical or hysterical about the times we're living in). Which isn't to say that camera movement isn't a continuing concern of Snow's cinema: consider, for starters, *Back and Forth*, *La région centrale*, *Breakfast*, and *Presents*—the latter of which pulls another version of the same stunt that I've tentatively attributed to Dreyer by moving the set rather than the camera, in this case with jerky, slapstick consequences.

4.
My review of Michelangelo Antonioni's *The Passenger** is one of my few published pieces that hasn't appeared on my website, probably due to an oversight, although in theory it might have once appeared there and then, accidentally or not, gotten erased. I'm not even sure if I agree with its argument now, half a century later, but because it deals with camera movement in search of identity, it seems appropriate to reproduce it here, in a book that I've deliberately cast adrift, forcing it to seek out its own identity or identities. The plot concerns a reporter in Africa who decides to assume the identity of a dead acquaintance.

Because the lengthy camera movement at the end of *The Passenger* aka *Profession: Reporter* seems to have been conceived under the metaphorical and metaphysical shadow of Snow's *Wavelength*, this seems to be the right place for its loitering drifts (as well as mine), even though today I'm more drawn towards considering the film as a form of architecture seen as landscape (or vice versa), graced and accommodated by a CinemaScope format. I've made only minor cosmetic changes apart from paragraphing. (In 1974, all of the *Monthly Film Bulletin*'s reviews were formatted in single paragraphs, preceded by single-paragraph synopses. The highly dubious premise then was that synopses were "objective," whereas reviews

---

* *Monthly Film Bulletin*, June 1975.

were "subjective," but I've omitted the synopsis in this case because I suspect that it only adds more confusion for readers who haven't seen the film.)

The problem is, Antonioni at his near-best bears a disturbing resemblance to Antonioni at his near-worst. (The same mannerist tendency towards blissful self-parody and take-it-or-leave-it bombast can be found in Faulkner's *Sanctuary, Absalom, Absalom* and *Pylon*; a prime example from *Pylon* can be found in this book's second prologue.) So my ambivalence about *The Passenger* is no doubt ascribable in part to its own detachable and less than symbiotic parts, whereby the characters don't become either serious enough or silly enough to sustain much interest or focus and the film gets confused with its original pitch or treatment, emerging as an academic treatise more than a story with characters we can care about.

> In a crumbling African village, David Locke [Jack Nicholson] asks for directions in faltering phrases ('Vous parlez français?') while the camera repeatedly pans away from him; in the desert, stranded in the sand with his land-rover, he sobs 'I don't care' while he is abandoned again by an indifferent camera drifting over empty dunes. Seemingly 'uncomposed' in terms of framing, dialogue, or discernible narrative direction, *The Passenger* charts the confusion of an identity going to pieces. The remainder of the film carries him from a new life as Robertson to an oddly fulfilling death in the same guise, when the camera once again turns away from him, this time to discover a richer (if no more legible) counterpart to his personality. His wife and producer are meanwhile left to collect and create a coherent version of his earlier self: 'If

you try hard enough, you can re-invent him,' someone remarks to Rachel, and her efforts run parallel to Locke's re-invention of Robertson. Near the end of the film's penultimate, seven-minute shot—a camera movement defining the hero's nemesis and apotheosis as it proceeds out his window and around the square, accumulating all the diverse threads of his destiny in a choreography of passing figures—after the camera has gradually swung back around to find him dead, a Spanish official asks Rachel and then the girl, 'Do you recognize him?' 'I never knew him,' Rachel replies, while the girl says 'Yes'; both answers implicitly fuse the identities of Locke and Robertson, for both women could be speaking about either one of them.

Working with a conception that is perhaps even more literary than the art-and-illusion conceit framing *Blow-Up*—with echoes of everything from Conrad's 'inscrutable' Africa to any number of Borges tales—Antonioni molds a specifically filmic intrigue by periodically disrupting the linear flow that his putative thriller plot suggests, thrusting the spectator into a mosaic of uncertainties increased by steady displacements in space and time.

While Locke sets about switching passport photos, a camera movement away from him accompanies an aural flashback (a conversation between him and Robertson) that becomes visual when the camera reaches a window (which frames the conversation); moving back toward Locke with the passports, the camera passes the turning reels of a tape recorder playing the conversation, which returns us to sound and image in the present tense. In the church in Munich where Locke is met by the African rebel emissaries, a cut between camera set-ups reveals that the 'funeral' taking place is in fact a wedding ceremony, while subsequent cuts transport us into a flashback followed by a flashforward, then obliquely back into the church (via Locke's feet stepping over flower petals), and later, into his interview with an African leader (with Locke off-screen), then into a London editing studio where Martin and Rachel are watching the sequence, and finally (over Rachel's voice) into a flashback of the interview being shot.

Continually redirecting our attention, *The Passenger* fragments and diverts its story to the point where it becomes even more cryptic once all its basic components and possibilities (both literal and symbolic) are reassembled in the climactic shot where—along with the hero and the Third World struggle he ambiguously relates to—it becomes an abstract generalization about identity rather than a concrete realization of its taking shape. The dissolution of character and identity into landscape is of course basic to Antonioni; one finds it implied in Anna's disappearance from the island in *L'avventura,* the conclusion of *Eclipse*, the elusive park murder in *Blow-Up*, the desert orgy and exploding ranch house in *Zabriskie Point*, and the picaresque walks taken by protagonists in most of the other films.

In *The Passenger,* this dissolution and displacement is once again associated with death, and there is a sense of completion as well as absence in Antonioni's delineation of it, once he takes leave of the competent naturalistic interactions between Nicholson and Maria Schneider (the latter a very appealing version of the resourceful Girl Friday out of *film noir*) to pursue a more abstract version of his theme. This departure is more than adequately prefigured by two signals in the preceding scene: Locke asking the girl [sic] to describe what she sees through another window in the room, and then telling her a rather bleak and portentous story about a blind man regaining his sight at the age of forty. Two rather self-conscious evocations of the birth-to-death cycle, these 'message carriers'—along with most of the film's intellectual and cultural baggage—bear a weight of significance that the film's finer moments dispense with entirely, moving away from the uncertainties of 'truth' and 'personality' and toward the even stranger certainties of a physical environment, with the sort of airborne relief that can only come from travelling light—that state of spiritual awakening explicitly sought by Locke when he first sets the plot in motion.

One key difference between the camera drifting away from the action in Radu Jude's *Bad Luck Banging or Loony Porn* (2021)—specifically away from the heroine's path as she walks through Bucharest—and the camera drifting away from Locke in *The Passenger* is that the former serves to expand the narrative by linking its fictional plot to a documentary exploration of its space, whereas in *The Passenger* the movement is a kind of contraction, bracketing every path not taken as a kind of denial of narrative itself. This shedding of possible narratives is supposed to serve as some sort of clarification for the narrative that remains, but I find it both cumbersome and confused as Locke wanders through portions of Africa hoping to regain his identity. The fact that he's little more than a theorem to begin with is largely what accounts for my disengagement.

In *Bad Luck Banging*, this wandering becomes part of the drift of the narrative; in *The Passenger*, it arguably *is* the drift. Indeed, most of Antonioni's films from *L'avventura* onwards resemble a certain form of tourism, entailing the sort of social detachment that would arguably play some part in fostering the controversial receptions of both *Zabriskie Point* (1970) and *Chung Kuo, Cina* (1972), the two features immediately preceding *The Passenger*, in the U.S. and China, respectively. Indeed, the major elements in *L'avventura* (1960), *La notte* (1961), *Eclipse* (1962) and *Red Desert* (1964) mitigating against their touristic distance from their plots are the characters and performances of their lead actors. The literary and metaphysical aspects of *Blow-up* (1966), on the other hand, help to complicate and disguise its touristic approach toward London. The fact that spectators are invited as tourists into the Italian worlds of *L'avventura*, *La notte*, *Eclipse* and *Red Desert*, in which movie stars (e.g., Monica Vitti, Jeanne Moreau, Marcello Mastroianni, Alain Delon) function as guides, makes it easier to overlook the extent to which these films also function as metaphysical parables. In short, one could argue that it's the tourism of *The Passenger*—combined with a use of Nicholson as another tourist that precludes him from functioning as a guide—that makes its status as a metaphysical parable overwhelm its other narrative agendas, turning all its characters, including Locke, into props. The film's alternate title, *Profession: Reporter*, highlights its metaphysics by turning Locke into a function whereas *The Passenger* conceals its metaphysics by equating the film's spectators with its hero. Thus the climactic slow camera movement away from Locke just before he dies—subverting our identification with his character and reducing his identity to what he means for other people—resurrects the disturbing sense of absence found in Antonioni's previous films, but this time without the outlines of a recognizable world informing such an absence.

Antonioni's sense of absence seems derived in part from the eerie, empty landscapes in paintings by Giorgio de Chirico, which are already metaphysical by definition. (The relevant canvases, painted between 1909 and 1919, are said to belong to de Chirico's "metaphysical period," reportedly stimulated by his reading of Nietzsche.) Predicated on a merging of "inner" (psychological) reality with "external" (physical) reality, as was Surrealism during the same period, this tendency seems closely allied with the ambiguity about agency in the camera movements of Phạm Thiên Ân's *Inside the Yellow Cocoon Shell* that I discussed in the first chapter, where it becomes impossible to distinguish its hero's movements from the movements of its narrative.

One of the most literal examples of Antonioni's Chirico influence occurs during a key sequence in *L'avventura* in which the romantic leads, Sandro (Gabriele Ferzetti) and Claudia (Monica Vitti), searching for the missing Anna (Sandro's mistress and Claudia's friend, played by Lea Massari), stop briefly in a deserted village. The sequence begins and ends with apparently unmotivated camera movements—a pan to the right that eventually reaches their moving car before it stops and they get out, and a slow, barely perceptible move forward as their car drives away in the distance. In both cases, the camera seems to linger on the uninhabited setting (whose emptiness is never explained), creating an uncanny effect that suggests an invisible witness—possibly Anna herself, possibly Antonioni—whose gaze seems to motivate the camera's otherwise gratuitous movement. The lack of any resolution to this mystery combines with the previous mysterious disappearance of Anna from a volcanic island that occasioned Sandro and Claudia's search for her to create a tension that is both moral and metaphysical: moral because Sandro and Claudia's evolving relationship suggests that they're both "cheating" on Anna (the sequence ends with a shock cut to them embracing at a subsequent location), and metaphysical because the reason for Anna's disappearance seems to evolve from being unexplained to being unexplainable.

In subsequent Antonioni films, this sort of moral tension is gradually overtaken by metaphysical doubts until moral ambiguity appears to vanish altogether in *The Passenger*—a development that for me limits the urgency of the metaphysical issues. Henceforth, I would argue, Antonioni's art cinema becomes arty and mannerist, as this filmmaker's detractors claimed it always was.

9
I LOVE THE RHYTHM IN A RIFF: HITCHCOCK'S PANS, COLLECTIVE AUTHORSHIP

Half a century ago, shortly after starting my new job as assistant editor at the *Monthly Film Bulletin* (at the British Film Institute in London), I compared Alfred Hitchcock to Jean Renoir in a review of Hitchcock's *Blackmail* (1929). The review, published in the October 1974 issue of the *Bulletin*, begins as follows:

> The extraordinary plateau attained by Hitchcock's first sound film in relation to his overall development is the sum of many accomplishments: above all, a decisive mastery in moving back and forth between objective and subjective narrative modes. If the point-of-view is one of the cornerstones in Hitchcockian syntax, the film quite likely represents the first time in the director's career that it is woven so seamlessly into a plot that all notions of stylistic "touches" give way to a sustained psychological density. Beginning virtually like a documentary, *Black-*

mail provides a quick foretaste of subjective truth in its early glimpses of the anonymous criminal, which subtly veer from the police's viewpoint to his own—shifting, that is, from one kind of fear and apprehension to another. The complex overtones and ambiguities of the film are informed throughout by this kind of duplicity and intimacy, which oblige us to identify with rapist along with potential victim, murderer along with corpse, and detective along with blackmailer, at the same time as we are asked to regard them all with a certain amused skepticism. The shifting trajectories composing the plot work hand in glove with the moral ambivalences. After taking us from police to criminal and back again, the film directs us to a single policeman (Frank [John Longden]), abandons him to trace his girlfriend's infidelity, invites us to "participate" in both her potential ravishment and her act of murder, then in her sense of guilt (starkly delineated in a neon sign, London streets at dawn, a beggar's outstretched hand, and the idle chatter of a neighbor—each brilliantly rendered as a subjective impression echoing the crime), next encourages us to identify with her *and* Frank when Tracy appears, only to shift to Tracy himself as he is hounded to his death, and at last reverting to the couple again. But even they are supplanted by the final image: the mocking face of a joker in one of the artist's paintings, making its last appearance as the police carry the canvas away. This leitmotif might recall (or anticipate) the sardonic disdain expressed for all the characters in Hitchcock's late work, but the irony here is never allowed to block compassion. It assumes as much a leavening as a leveling function, often ridiculing heroes and humanizing villains in single strokes—as in the cut from the satisfied police inspector ordering Tracy's arrest to Tracy himself, seen in an identical posture and looking equally satisfied as he polishes off a free meal served by Alice. Such equations (and the film has many) suggest a moral framework similar to that in subsequent films by Renoir, where everyone has his own reasons.

Lamentably missing from this final comparison is any recognition that Hitchcock is being judgmental toward his characters in a way that Renoir is not and that the shifts in perspective are most often made via pans from one character to another. These two missing elements are interconnected if we acknowledge that the pans are not statements of moral equivalence but statements of equivalent weights and parallel subjectivities, perceived as the two sides of a weighing scale.

The film opens with a police van racing across London to pick up a suspect for an undisclosed crime, and the first pan is a dizzying subjective sweep across the street from the viewpoint of the van's passengers. A suggestion of parallel events is already introduced when these police subsequently enter a building and cross a courtyard, and the hyperactive scampering of boys playing in both locations creates a rhyme effect with the movements of the cops. Then the film's first pan across an interior moves from the suspect, lying on his bed and reading a newspaper, to a mirrored reflection of cops entering his room to apprehend him as actual or suspected criminal.

The "transference of guilt" theme identified in Hitchcock's films by the *Cahiers du Cinéma* gang during the 1950s is especially evident here, in his first talkie, where a petty criminal attempting to blackmail the heroine (who murdered a painter trying to rape her) is in effect "blackmailed" in turn by her detective boyfriend, who turns the blackmailer into a prime suspect for the murder that she committed.

Panning back and forth between two characters is a trope that can also be found in diverse films of the *nouvelle vague*, especially Godard's *Le mépris* (1963), where the movements are between Michel Piccoli and Brigitte Bardot. In some ways it resembles a game of catch between opponents, at least if one can imagine replacing a ball with not so much a camera as a camera's gaze. Hitchcock implicitly makes it a judgmental gaze.

o o o

Some of what follows is derived, developed, and revised from "Visionary Agitprop" in *The Chicago Reader*, December 8, 1995, and "Identity Politics" (a review of *I Am Cuba, Siberian Mammoth*, a Brazilian documentary about *I Am Cuba*) in *The Chicago Reader*, April 11, 2005.

Undeniably monstrous and breathtakingly beautiful, ridiculous and awe inspiring, *I Am Cuba* confounds so many usual yardsticks of judgment that any kind of rating becomes inadequate. A delirious, lyrical, epic piece of communist propaganda from 1964—at least three years in the making and 141 minutes long—it is simply too campy and too grotesque to qualify as a "masterpiece," but I'd probably care less about it if it were one.

A Russian-Cuban production, it reportedly was hated in Russia and Cuba alike in the mid-1960s, at least among government officials; in Cuba it was commonly known as *I Am Not Cuba*. Apparently it wasn't seen anywhere else until the 1992 Telluride film festival, where an unsubtitled print was shown as part of a tribute to director Mikhail Kalatozov.

It was subsequently presented jointly by Francis Ford Coppola and Martin Scorsese, but one can't readily lump it with the other art-house classics that they've helped to distribute. It does frequently remind one of two celebrated unfinished features about Latin America by gifted outsiders, Sergei Eisenstein's *Que Viva Mexico* (studied by the director and writers of *I Am Cuba* during preproduction) and Orson Welles' *It's All True* (unavailable for study until recently). But since these films were never completed they don't define a tradition this movie can belong to; at most they suggest the sort of sensual fantasies foreigners are apt to have about South Americans and Central Americans. Started before the Cuban missile crisis, *I Am Cuba* also harks back to such episodic revolutionary epics as Eisenstein's *Battleship Potemkin* and Pudovkin's *Deserter*, as well as to historically inspired portmanteau features like Rossellini's *Paisan*. But the baroque style of *I Am Cuba* may ultimately and paradoxically come closer to that of Disney's *The Three Caballeros*, made in 1945.

It's far from certain that Mikhail Kalatozov, the credited director, is the individual most responsible for the film's distinctiveness. Judging from its unique, shimmering black-and-white look and the testimony of its co-writer, Russian poet Yevgeny Yevtushenko, the film belongs mainly to its cinematographer, the extraordinary Sergei Urusevsky (1908–1974), but I have no way of confirming this impression. (Urusevsky shot the two other Kalatozov films I've seen, *The Cranes Are Flying* from 1957 and *The Letter Never Sent* from 1960, the second a hallucinatory tale about four geologists hunting for diamonds in the Siberian taiga that's said to have influenced Andrei Tarkovsky and the Coppola of *Apocalypse Now*; *The Letter Never Sent* was roundly criticized by its production unit as formalist, though it still packs a punch.)

A couple of other oddities about *I Am Cuba* are worth noting—one linguistic, the other visual. The dialogue and narration are mainly in Spanish, apart from a few lines in English (coming mainly from characters designated as American tourists and sailors). There's also a Russian voice-over that translates the Spanish and English, and English subtitles that translate the Russian and Spanish, with the result that most of the English lines you hear are different from the ones you read: when an American tourist in a decadent Havana nightclub says "I'll take a limeade," this is duly translated into Russian, and the Russian line is then subtitled "A soft drink for me."

The visual style closely resembles Orson Welles' in many particulars: low and canted angles, lengthy and highly expressive camera movements, high-contrast chiaroscuro, and the use of a wide-angle lens to create spatial distortion in the foregrounds of shots and deep focus in the backgrounds. Yet if one compares *I Am Cuba* to the feature that Welles was making in Europe at the same time, *The Trial* (1962), the differences in meaning are vast. There's a much closer match between *I Am Cuba* and Welles' 1958 *Touch of Evil*—ironically a film denounced in Russia for its "decadence," most notably by director Sergei Yutkevich. In part this resemblance can be attributed to the fact that all of the action in *Touch of Evil* is set in and around a Mexican border town; and if one compares the use in both pictures of a jazzy kind of rock music to suggest corruption and seediness, one might even say that their puritanical responses to malfeasance are quite similar.

The parallels between Welles' camera style and *I Am Cuba*'s are especially intriguing from an ideological standpoint. Welles remained a leftist (mainly of the currently disparaged "liberal" variety) throughout his career, yet most popular appreciations of his work,

Citizen Kane in particular, tend to be right-wing celebrations of headstrong individualism—an individualism in which an expressive camera style is always read as personal, individualized expression triumphing over collective effort. The fact that the notorious formalism of *I Am Cuba* was attacked in both Cuba and Russia in the 1960s might suggest that it's actually a conservative movie in disguise. But it's much likelier that our Yankee capitalist reflexes may force us to read collective work in individualist auteurist terms even when they don't apply and give up on a puzzle like *I Am Cuba* when it fails to yield the usual auteurist rewards.

Let's start with the aforementioned sense of decadence near the beginning of *I Am Cuba*, which makes such a strong impression that the remainder of the movie never quite recovers from it. Our first taste of it comes after a couple of gorgeous sequences introduce us briefly to the topography of Cuba and to some poor people living in a village. The second sequence is a veritable theme-park ride down a picturesque tropical stream with a boatman, past huts on stilts where children play and women wash their clothes, and it introduces us to a formalism that more or less remains operative throughout the remainder of the picture, quickly becoming its most troubling and fascinating aspect. After this sequence there's an abrupt cut to a jazzy rock band blasting away on a rooftop overlooking the Havana beaches while numerous bathing beauties stroll by—the basic material for a breathtaking sequence without any cuts—followed by a sequence purportedly set in a Havana nightclub. In both of these extended accounts of Yankee corruption during the late Batista period the film is as two-faced as Larry Clark's *Kids* in clucking its tongue at the nasty revels it can't get enough of. If anything, it's even more appreciative of what it's showing than Clark's film—which makes it more fun to look at, though harder to process as any sort of communist movie. As the camera moves several stories down to applauding tourists around an outdoor swimming pool — lingering over a pretty blond woman in a dress who's being handed a drink, then abandoning her to follow a poolside bathing beauty into the water — we're clearly on another theme-park ride. Then, when the camera (and the accompanying sound) goes even further and dips with the bather below the water's surface, we're arguably entering a realm closer to the sex-crazed cartoons of Tex Avery. Back in 1965, Urusevsky tried to justify this delirious move thematically in relation to the previous village sequence: "Taking the camera into the pool is justified because water is the visual link between the two scenes," he wrote. But Urusevsky's literary analogy isn't very convincing because this second theme-park excursion, unlike the first, celebrates festive opulence rather than everyday populism.

We next move to the nightclub, where Ignacio — the falsetto lead for the Platters during the 1950s — is singing in Spanish about "this crazy love in my blood." A den of iniquity whose bamboo poles suggest prison bars and whose large wooden idols make us think of barbaric rites, this nightmarish cavern with its elaborate Afro-Cuban floor show and prostitutes at the bar introduces us to three male tourists implausibly identified as Americans. The most prominent of these, Jim, who has a fetish for crucifixes, is played by the French actor Jean Bouise, later known for his performances in *La guerre est finie*, *The Conformist*, *Out 1* and *Z*.

In a subsequent sequence we see Jim take one of the prostitutes back to her shack in the Havana ghetto (a hut that oddly resembles a gigantic Russian constructivist sculpture); in the morning he insists on purchasing her crucifix, which she doesn't want to sell. As he walks away through the crowded ghetto, accompanied by the sound of a humming male voice and a solo guitar, the tilted camera, starting from a birdcage he passes, cranes up the full height of a telephone pole, while a woman designated as the "voice of Cuba" in the credits intones, "I am Cuba. Why are you leaving? You came here to have fun. Go ahead, have fun! Isn't this a happy picture? Don't avert your eyes. Look, I am Cuba. For you, I am the casino, the bar, the hotels and brothels. But the hands of these children and old people are also me. I am Cuba."

In current economic parlance, one might argue that *I Am Cuba* doesn't belong in our cultural vocabulary because it invests all its aesthetic capital in a bad business venture. I guess that means it must be wrong, no matter how good it looks. One might even say that the "bad business" in this case is the collective coordination needed to make a lengthy camera movement even more extended, so that it not only depicts a crowd of people but also requires several other people to realize its depiction, thus confounding the implicit Yankee auteurist bias that a camera movement is the expression of a single artist, not a collective team working interactively. In short, the title of this film really should have been *We Are Cuba*, especially because the first-person singular corresponds to what we see and hear only when the story concerns defeat.

There are three more extended sequences in *I Am Cuba*. The first, a clear exposition of the aforementioned defeat, shows us a sugarcane harvester learning that his brutal boss has sold his land to the United Fruit Company and that he has to vacate his house. Sending his son and daughter into town, he burns the sugarcane field and his house to the ground before collapsing in despair. (The third and least memorable extended sequence follows various rebel soldiers fighting and regrouping in the mountains as well as one peasant family dodging bombs and seeing their home demolished; the husband tells his family he has to join the rebel forces and winds up singing the Cuban national anthem with them.)

The second extended sequence pivots from singular defeat to collective solidarity. In Havana we follow the adventures of Enrique, a radical student who saves a woman from a band of drunken American sailors, reads in the paper that Fidel Castro is dead, meets with his comrades, and prepares to assassinate a fat police officer who has killed many of his friends, though he loses his nerve at the last minute. Then the police raid a room where students are printing pro-Castro leaflets, and one of the protesters is shot. A crowd gathers, and Enrique addresses it until another shot rings out and a white dove falls. Holding the dead bird aloft like a flag, Enrique leads the crowd, now singing the Cuban national anthem, into the street, where they're met with water hoses.

Shot by the fat cop, Enrique then becomes a revolutionary martyr. His coffin is carried by his comrades through downtown Havana, surrounded by a crowd that swells to Cecil B. DeMille proportions. In a delirious, breathtaking two-and-a-half-minute shot, the camera moves ahead of a young woman and then past a young man— catching him in closeup as he turns around, hoists the front of the coffin onto his right shoulder, and walks away with the other pallbearers. The camera then cranes up the five floors of a building, past countless people watching from balconies and parapets, before it moves to the right across the street and through a window into a cigar-rolling factory, where it follows workers as they hand a Cuban flag one to another, eventually unfurling it from another window. The camera next moves out that window and over the flag, and then follows the funeral cortege from above for what seems like a good quarter of a mile. (A partial explanation of how this astonishing shot was achieved is offered by the cameraman, Alexander Calzatti, in the July 1995 issue of *American Cine-*

matographer; it required a "special cable device" that Calzatti built in Moscow before coming to Cuba.)

In *I Am Cuba, Siberian Mammoth,* Vicente Ferraz's 2004 Brazilian documentary about the making of *I Am Cuba,* after we're shown this spectacular black-and-white shot, Ferraz offers a color shot of a Cuban man on the same street today recalling what a great shot it was. But significantly, he doesn't even remember that he was the young man who turned around in closeup while lifting the coffin, until Ferraz reminds him of this fact.

This man may have been the most prominent individual in one of the most spectacular shots in film history, yet his inability to remember this forty years later speaks volumes about what it means to be inside a revolutionary movement. That the funeral was either fictional or restaged for the camera is secondary, because we learn that for this man in the mid-1960s, being part of the Cuban revolution and being part of *I Am Cuba* were separate aspects of the same experience. He makes clear that it was the collective moment that mattered then, not his individual participation in it.

Throughout much of the film Urusevsky and his skilled camera crew (three of whom are billed in the credits simply for "pyrotechnics") use infrared film stock that makes palm trees and sugarcane look as white as sun-soaked sheets—an astonishing visual effect that mythologizes the Cuban landscape, making it an appropriate setting for dreams. An estimated 97 percent of the film was shot with handheld cameras, and though the early rooftop sequence may seem to be the work of one frenzied individual, it was actually carried out by a relay team of three separate camera operators—a good example of collective work that can't begin to mesh with any auteurist premise of a camera representing the will of a single director who "produces" whatever we see onscreen. In fact, much of the handheld camera work throughout feels personal without being individualized, an apt reflection of the film's poetic and political agendas.

In an unfinished 1955 essay re-evaluating Russian silent films by Eisenstein, Pudovkin, and Dovzhenko, Robert Warshow found these films reprehensible because of their aesthetic distinction. Given the frequent American mistrust of art, it's a telling confession, all the more notable for coming from a critic whose grasp of aesthetics was more sophisticated than most of his colleagues. "It was not at all an aesthetic failure that I encountered in these movies," he wrote, "but something much worse: a triumph of art over humanity. It made me, for a while, quite sick of the art of the cinema, and sick also of those people who sat with me in the audience, *mes semblables*, whom I suspected of being either cinema enthusiasts or Communists—and I wasn't always sure which was worse."*

He could have been writing about *I Am Cuba*— a triumph of art over humanity, he might have added, except that it evidently wasn't regarded as any sort of triumph when it appeared in Cuba and Russia sixty years ago. Yet given that art is a human activity that isn't practiced by insects, capitalist censorship—a near-constant in our lives that we're generally trained to ignore or misrepresent—prevents us from coming to terms with *I Am Cuba* in any coherent or consistent fashion. It isn't precisely "un film de Mikhail Kalatozov" or any other individual but a team effort inspired by a collective utopian vision, and even though its contrived fictions periodically border on the absurd, none of its misrepresentations begin to exonerate the corruptions of Batista and his American customers. We can't swallow its hyperbole or come up with any alternative to it, so we auto-

---

* Robert Warshow, "Re-Viewing the Russian Movies" in *The Immediate Experience* (Harvard, 2001), 241-42.

matically tune out of its discourse, most often without any clear acknowledgment of what we're rejecting.

Insofar as *I Am Cuba* celebrates collective endeavors, it depicts revolution as something achievable in terms of pyrotechnics, yet apparently neither Russians nor Cubans in the early 1960s were prone to support or endorse this attitude. Even so, it continues to offer an implied rebuke to the auteur-based model of art cinema that's ruled the West since the 1960s. Everyone Ferraz interviewed for his documentary described *I Am Cuba* as a collaborative venture—one can't credit its virtuosity, style, or content simply to director Mikhail Kalatozov or cinematographer Sergei Urusevsky or writers Yevgeny Yevtushenko and Enrique Pineda Barnet, as Western critics are wont to do. Ferraz's documentary also makes clear that there was another significant creative voice in the mix, Urusevsky's wife, Bella Friedman, the first assistant director and apparently the key figure linking the Russian and Cuban workers on the film. Even the Western tendency to associate a style of camera movement with one individual's sensibility is challenged, because the camera was sometimes relayed between crew members over the course of a single shot.

It seems both facile and ironic that Ferraz summarizes *I Am Cuba*'s current reputation by using ad copy. Hyperbolic adjectives are plastered over the documentary's VHS and DVD cases, one adjective per publication: "beautiful" from *New York* magazine, "exquisite" from the *LA Weekly*, "ecstatic" from the *Washington Post*, "dazzling" from *Interview*, and so on. One person whom Ferraz interviews in the film remarks that *I Am Cuba* was shunned when it was needed and celebrated only after it became a museum piece. He has a point, though it wouldn't be hard to make the same point about *Citizen Kane*. But given that *Citizen Kane* has been the standard bearer for auteurism since the 1960s, it's far more interesting that I *Am Cuba*'s alleged "Wellesian" style and sense of bravura aren't the result of any one individual's effort.

9
A NON-CONCLUSIVE EPILOGUE (*CUADECUC, VAMPIR*): WHAT A DIFFERENCE A PAN MAKES

It's possible that you've never heard of Pere Portabella's *Cuadecuc, Vampir* (1971) unless, perhaps, you've read my *Village Voice* Cannes coverage from 1971* and/or seen discussions of it in my 2010 book *Goodbye Cinema, Hello Cinephilia* and/or my 2024 book *In Dreams Begin Responsibilities*.

If, on the other hand, you've read any or all of the above texts, you might be confused that I reviewed a film in 1971 called simply *Vampir* by someone whose first name was Pedro, that in 2010 this became Pere Portabella's *Vampir-Cuadecuc* and was dated 1970, and that it was subsequently called both *Cuadecuc, Vampir* and *Vampir*.

What makes its identity so slippery? Portabella and his film's title are Catalan, an illegal language and forbidden ethnic identity in 1971 Spain, and regardless

---

* "Moviegoing at Cannes: Classics without Labels," *The Village Voice*, June 17, 1971. Also available at https://jonathanrosenbaum.net/2023/12/moviegoing-at-cannes-classics-without-labels. Nothing is very certain these days, but the last time I checked, one could access this movie (or is it this film?) for free at https://ok.ru/video/2326766422734, or else purchase it on Blu-ray from diverse sources.

of what it's called, it isn't generally considered part of—or authorized by—the film industry, which directly or indirectly defines what we usually mean by film history. The only screenings it received in Spain under General Francisco Franco's rule, if it had any at all, were clandestine. So what we call it and how we regard it is largely a matter of shifting circumstances. In fact, one of the shots I alluded to in my 1971 review ("a ghoulishly made-up actress making a face at someone between takes") is no longer part of the film.

In all its manifestations, it's a silent documentary about a commercial film being shot in Barcelona (Jesús Franco's 1969 *Count Dracula*), except for when it enters *Count Dracula*'s scenes like a handheld Brakhage camera scouring a scene for flesh, or else ambles away from those scenes to explore various "offscreen" effects (e.g., where the onscreen mist or cobwebs are coming from). You also might say that the documentary periodically seems to become part of the fiction of *Count Dracula*. Like any hapless citizen in an occupied country, it has to work both sides of the street simply in order to stay alive.

The shots are sometimes edited together "unprofessionally" and discontinuously, as if they were fragments in an unfinished documentary. And when some of these shots include a pan, we can't be sure if the pan originates from Jesús Franco and his 35mm cinematographer or from Portabella and his 16mm cinematographer. Maybe it derives from both, and we might wind up concluding that life is like that, experienced either as a haphazard pile of one damned thing on top of another or else as an orderly procession, and we might decide that we like the procession more because it's more fluid—more "panny," so to speak. Which is another way of saying that the film is curious and not at all embarrassed or ashamed about its curiosity. So panning is another way of pursuing mysteries, accompanied by a *musique concrète* soundtrack by Carles Santos (1940–2017) that tends to expand our uncertainties rather than resolve them.

Indeed, the film as a whole can be perceived as an ongoing, interactive duet between Portabella and Santos, often witty and ironic in its juxtapositions. And pans from the film being shot to various peripheral details are a basic part of its rhythm and its subject. To state this somewhat differently, what is or isn't peripheral is part of what the film investigates, and its peripheral status of the film itself in relation to both history and film history is part of its concern.

Cuadecuc rudely and abruptly assaults us at the outset by starting right in the goddam middle of a camera movement, in black and white, chasing after a horse-drawn carriage that's crossing an ancient city square under a steady drizzle, an image that registers as historical and immediate in equal measure—to which Santos offers a matching explosive lurch that hits us like a solid shove forward on the soundtrack. Already we're being bumped about, we know not where or why, except that it's being drummed into us that life is abrupt motion and scattered focus, some of which gets translated into a series of pans, habitual exercises in restlessness, all driven by the command to keep everything in motion—everything, that is, except for the boilerplate Bram Stoker *Dracula* plot, which keeps getting tripped over as a distracting encumbrance as much as a connecting thread. All we can be sure of is that the horse-drawn carriage is trotting through a drizzle and the camera is suddenly lurching in relation to that, making us all feel like guinea pigs in some unnamed and undisclosed mad-scientist experiment.

What makes these simple camera movements, mostly pans, profoundly yet offhandedly radical are their switches and shifts in syntax between story and setting that seem analogous to the mid-sentence jolts and unexpected attachments/collisions of Brion Gysin and William S. Burroughs' cutups, jamming together two randomly chosen and unconnected pages of text to see what gets produced by the chance encounter. The analogy I have in mind is metaphysical, insofar as it might be said that Portabella commits the physical act of jamming together two unrelated texts and discourses in order to escape physicality entirely.

Portabella himself, I hasten to add, is commonly ignored by film criticism and film history alike as they're usually recounted and recorded, unlike hack filmmaker Franco, for reasons that are neither artistic nor social but, arguably, industrial. This is simply because Franco, unlike Portabella, belongs to the film industry and therefore is worthy of cult worship. Portabella, by contrast, can only pose questions rather than answer them, which keeps him firmly beyond the pale. (In 1972, *Variety*'s Spanish correspondent responded to my mention of Portabella as if I'd just uttered an obscenity.)

One might say that every time that Portabella pans anywhere in *Cuadecuc*, the same confounding existential questions hover over that moment like clouds casting shadows: Such as, am I watching a documentary, joining a fiction, joining a documentary, watching a fiction, or passing back and forth between all four of these options like a restless insect? And, are we supposed to be in the 19th century at this particular instant, or is it the 20th, or maybe the 21st? And how can we be sure of which century it might be until after we've answered the first question? Furthermore, because the questions themselves are a bit like pans, and vice versa, we also have to question and clarify our own limitations as classifiers of Portabella pans. As Julien Allen wrote recently in the online *Reverse Shot*: "The effect is of the film becoming unbound from its subject and pressing on, like the phantom carriage itself: not possessed, but free to float and drift where it will, and to take our inquisitive souls with it."*

To pan briefly from *Cuadecuc, Vampir* to Portabella himself, I was unable to meet him when he premiered *Vampir*, his second feature, at Cannes because the Spanish government of Francisco Franco (1892–1975) had confiscated his passport as punishment for his having been one of the two Spanish producers of Luis Buñuel's *Viridiana*, which had shared Cannes' Palme d'or in 1961.

But at Portabella's initiative, and with his secretary serving as mutual interpreter, we became occasional penpals over the next half-century and eventually met at events relating to his work in New York, Chicago, London, and Cambridge. While I was still living in Paris, he arranged for me to meet Carles Santos there, and a couple of decades later he got a daughter of his to look me up in Chicago. He also contributed a 5900-word "Prologue" to the 2010 Spanish edition of *Movie Mutations*, an international collection that I had launched and coedited over a decade earlier. (His secretary also kindly sent me a copy of this book after the Spanish publisher failed to do so.)

For Spaniards who know Portabella as a wealthy arts patron and a former post-Franco state senator who helped to abolish the death penalty and smooth Spain's pathway into the European Union, it is Portabella's profile as a filmmaker that's peripheral. For me, it's largely the reverse, so what I keep returning to are the radical thrusts *of Cuadecuc, Vampir* and *Umbracle* during the Franco freeze, the careful groundwork for living in a post-Franco world in *General Report* (1977), and, finally, the spectacular, festive Portabella films, both utopian celebrations, including my second favorite of his features, *Warsaw Bridge* (1990), and the equally multicultural and jubilant *The Silence Before Bach* (2007).

---

* https://reverseshot.org/features/3277/pumpkins_xix.

(I've refrained from mentioning his complete filmography in order to focus on what I value the most.) Both the man and his work illustrate the enduring virtues of not knowing where you belong—a state of being which makes camera movement a form of unresolved self-definition, better known as a search.

ACKNOWLEDGEMENTS

This book was inaugurated by an invitation from Erika Balsom to contribute a volume to a series called Cutaways that she was coediting with Genevieve Yue for Fordham University Press. encouraging me to make it "experimental." Although she, Genevieve and Thomas Lay (an in-house editor at Fordham) approved my choice of topic, our preferences began to diverge when it came to their accepting my title, and other differences arose after I submitted my manuscript, some of which related to my viewing the book, for better or for worse, in literary terms more than as an academic study. (Having suffered some exploitation as an adjunct in film studies programs during the 70s and 80s due to my failure to acquire the right degrees, I've also had some mixed experiences with other academic presses, two of which rejected my 2024 collection *In Dreams Begin Responsibilities* because their publicists had more clout than their editors.) Although I tried to make some suggested revisions on *Camera Movements That Confound Us*, my concurrent work on a book-length interview for Sticking Place Books eventually persuaded me that they would be a more suitable press for the more eccentric book I had in mind, and I'm especially grateful to Paul Cronin for making this possible, as well as to Erika, Genevieve and Tom for their own helpful suggestions before I made the switch. (It was thanks to Genevieve, for instance, that I discovered the wondrous *Inside the Yellow Cocoon Shell*.) These four people, as well as some anonymous readers at both presses, all played significant roles in helping me with this book, although needless to say, the faults, provocations and potential irritations are strictly and exclusively mine.

Jonathan Rosenbaum
Spring 2025

INDEX

8½ (Fellini), 65-66
12 Angry Men (Rose), 50-51
25th Hour (Lee), 39
2001: A Space Odyssey (Kubrick), 39

Abel, Alfred, 59
Absalom, Absalom (Faulkner), 89
A House is Not a Home: Wright or Wrong (Saeed-Vafa), 6
Akerman, Chantal, 4
Albertazzi, Giorgio, 31
Allen, Julien, 114
All the Memory in the World (Resnais), 32, 74-75, 77
Altman, Robert, 4, 63-66
American Cinematographer, 106
Amour à mort, L' (Resnais), 79, 82
Amour, fou, L' (Rivette), 62, 86
Antonioni, Michelangelo, 44, 88-95
Apocalypse Now (Coppola), 101
À propos de Nice (Vigo), 37-38
Arden, Robert, 30-31
Arditi, Pierre, 78, 81
Astruc, Alexandre, 7
Avery, Tex, 104
Avventura, L' (Antonioni), 91-94
Axelrod, George, 48
Azema, Sabine, 78, 81

Bad Luck Banging (Jude), 92-93
Back and Forth (Snow), 88
Balhaus, Michael, 23

Bardot, Brigitte, 100
Barnet, Enrique Pineda, 109
Band Wagon, The (Minnelli), 36
Barry Lyndon (Kubrick), 21
Barthes, Roland, 42
Basic, Count, 18
Battleship Potemkin (Eisenstein), 101
Bazin, André, 73
Beethoven, Ludwig van, 45
Benjamin, Walter, 54
Bergstrom, Janet, 24-25, 60
Bernstein, Henri, 78
Bigger Than Life (Ray), 68
Big Sky, The (Hawks), 20
Blackmail (Hitchcock), 97-100
Blow-Up (Antonioni), 90-91, 93
Böhm, Karlheinz, 22-23
Bordwell, David, 29
Bouise, Jean, 104
Boyer, Charles, 82
Brackett, Leigh, 64
Brakhage, Stan, 112
Breakfast (Snow), 88
Breathless (Godard), 6
Brecht, Bertolt, 45-46
Bresson, Robert, 16
Brick and Mirror (Golestan), 75-76
Broadway Scandals (Archainbaud), 68
Buñuel, Luis, 115
Burch, Noël, 29
Burroughs, William S., 114

Caballeros Three, The (Disney), 38, 101
Cahiers du Cinéma, 29, 42, 73, 99
Calzatti, Alexander, 106-107
Caniff, Milton, 80
Carstensen, Margit, 22
Casa de Lava (Costa), 34
Castro, Fidel, 106
Céline et Julie vont en bateau (Rivette), 49, 62
Chandler, Raymond, 64
Chaos as Usual (Lorenz), 23
Chaplin, Charles, 69
Chung Kuo, Cina (Antonioni), 93
Circle, The (Panahi), 53
Cissé, Souleymane, 81
Citizen Kane (Welles), 14, 69, 85, 102, 109
Clark, Larry, 103
Cocteau, Jean, 16
Collier, John, 53
Collins, Gail, 11
Comedian, The (Frankenheimer), 48, 50-51
Condon, Richard, 48
Conformist, The (Bertolucci), 104
Conrad, Joseph, 34, 90
Coppola, Francis Ford, 101
Costa, Pedro, 34-35
Coulouris, George, 85
Count Dracula (Franco), 112
Coutard, Raoul, 6
Cranes Are Flying, The (Kalatozov), 101
Crime of Monsieur Lange, The (Renoir), 41
Crown Jewels of Iran, The (Golestan), 75, 80
Crying of Lot 49, The (Pynchon), 33
Cuadecuc, Vampir (Portabella), 111-115
Cummings, Robert, 51

Dana, Jorge, 29
Dark Passage (Daves), 17
Daves, Delmer, 17
Day of Wrath (Dreyer), 28-30, 33, 36, 86
de Chirico, Giorgio, 94

Delon, Alain, 93
de Medeiros, Inês, 35
DeMille, Cecil B., 12, 106
De Palma, Brian, 21
de Putti, Lya, 59
Deserter (Pudovkin), 101
Disney, Walt 12, 37-38, 101
Dostoevsky, Fyodor, 41
Dovzhenko, Alexander, 108
Dreyer, Carl, 5-6, 21, 30, 33-34, 86, 88
Dr. Jekyll and Mr. Hyde (Mamoulian), 17
Dumbo (Disney), 37-38
Duperey, Anny, 82
Duras, Marguerite, 75
Durgnat, Ray, 41-42
Dussollier, André, 78

Earrings of Madame de..., The (Ophüls), 14
Eastwood, Clint, 46
Eclipse (Antonioni), 93
Eisenstein, Sergei, 101
Equinox Flower (Ozu), 69

Farahani, Mitra, 82
Fassbinder, Rainer Werner, 22-23
Faulkner, William, 2, 8-9, 34, 42-42
Faust (Murnau), 38
Fellini, Federico, 44, 65-66
Fendt, Ted, 42
Ferraz, Vicente, 107, 109
Ferzetti, Gabriele, 94
Film Comment, 68
Film Dope, 41
Final Chord (Sirk), 44-45
First Legion, The (Sirk), 42
Flaubert, Gustave, 4
Fonda, Henry, 51
Ford, John, 12, 69
Fountain of Youth, The (Welles), 52-53
Frampton, Hollis, 87
Franco, Francisco, 112, 115
Franco, Jesús, 112, 114
Frankenheimer, John, 48-50
Friedman, Bella, 109
Fuller, Samuel, 29, 51

Gaugin (Resnais), 74
Gaynor, Janet, 24
Gégauff, Paul, 83
General Report... (Portabella), 115
Gertrud (Dreyer), 29, 33, 36, 86
Gielgud, John, 53
Gigi (Minnelli), 74
Gilda (Vidor), 14, 74
Godard, Jean-Luc, 6, 16, 29, 36, 73-74, 81-82
Goodbye Cinema, Hello Cinephilia (Rosenbaum), 111
Golestan, Ebrahim, 75-76, 80-82
Gone with the Wind (Fleming), 30
Greer, Jane, 29
Gregory, James, 49
Grémillon, Jean, 44
Guerre est finie, La (Resnais), 104
Gunn, Dan, 34
Gysin, Brion, 114

Hasumi, Shiguéhiko, 67, 69-71
Hauptmann, Gerhart, 59
Haut bas fragile (Rivette), 41
Hawks, Howard, 19-20
Hayden, Sterling, 20
Henry Fonda for President (Horwath), 54-57
Henze, Hans Werner, 80-81
Hiroshima mon amour (Resnais), 29, 75, 77
Hitchcock, Alfred, 13, 21-22, 37, 97-100
Hitler, Adolf, 37-38
Hoffman, Philip Seymour, 39
Horwath, Alexander, 54
Hudson, Rock, 43

I Am Cuba (Kalatozov), 100-109
I Am Cuba, Siberian Mammoth (Ferraz), 100, 107
Imitation of Life (Sirk), 45
Ince, Thomas, 69
In Dreams Begin Responsibilities (Rosenbaum), 111
Ingram, Rex, 69
Inside the Yellow Cocoon Shell (Phạm), 35, 94
Invitation to Phantom (Bergstrom), 60

It's All True (Welles), 101
I Was Born, But... (Ozu), 70

Jamal, Ahmad, 18
Jannings, Emil, 62
Jean Renoir (Sesonske), 42
Jude, Radu, 92

Kalatozov, Mikhail, 100-101, 108
Kiarostami, Abbas, 82
Kids (Clark), 103
Killing, The (Kubrick), 20
Kortner, Fritz, 40-41
Krasznahorkai, László, 34
Kubrick, Stanley, 4, 20-21

Lady in the Lake, The (Montgomery), 17
Land of the Pharaohs (Hawks), 20
Lansbury, Angela, 49
Last Tycoon, The (Frankenheimer), 51
Last Year at Marienbad (Resnais), 6, 14, 31, 36., 49, 74-75, 77, 81
Lê, Phong Vũ, 35
Letter Never Sent, The (Kalatozov), 101
Letzte Mann, Der (Murnau), 61
Light in August (Faulkner), 34
Livingston, Margaret, 24
Longden, John, 98
Long Goodbye, The (Altman), 63-66
Looney Porn (Jude), 92
Lorenz, Juliane, 23
Losey, Joseph, 44
Love Unto Death (Resnais), 80-81
Lubitch, Ernst, 82
Lumet, Sidney, 51

Maddow, Rachel, 11
Magnificent Amberson, The (Welles), 14
Malick, Terrence, 13
Malone, Dorothy, 43
Mamoulian, Rouben, 13, 1747
Mann, Anthony, 51
Manchurian Candidate, The (Frankenheimer),
Mankiewicz, Joseph L., 13

March, Fredric, 17
Marker, Chris, 77, 81
Martha (Fassbinder), 22-23
Martin, Adrian, 32
Massari, Lea, 94
Mastroianni, Marcello, 93
McCarthy, Joseph, 49
McCarthy, Mary, 16-18, 20
Mélo (Resnais), 77, 79, 81-82
Melody of a Street Organ (Muratova), 65
Mépris, Le (Godard), 100
Mercer, David, 53
Metropolis (Lang), 59
MGM, 74, 81
Michelson, Annette, 87
Million Dollar Baby (Eastwood), 46
Mitchum, Robert, 29-30
Mizoguchi, Kenji, 13, 70
Monk, Thelonious, 18
Monkey Business (Hawks), 20
Monroe, Marilyn, 40
Montgomery, Robert, 17
Monthly Film Bulletin, 88, 97
Moorehead, Agnes, 85
Moreau, Jeanne, 93
Morgan, Daniel, 3, 14, 18
Moullet, Luc, 29, 42, 45
Mozart, Wolfgang Amadeus, 83
Mr. Arkadin/Confidential Report (Welles), 30, 61, 85
Muratova, Kira, 4, 13, 65-66
Murderer Dimitri Karamazov, The (Ozep), 40
Muriel (Resnais), 76, 80
Murnau. F. W., 4, 23-27, 38, 59-62

Nashville (Altman), 63
Nietzsche, Friedrich, 94
Nicholson, Jack, 89, 92-93
Night and Fog (Resnais), 32, 74-75
Nosferatu (Murnau), 59
Nostromo (Conrad), 34
Not on the Lips (Resnais), 74
Notte, La (Antonioni), 93
Novak, Kim, 21

O'Brien, George, 24, 26
Only Angels Have Wings (Hawks), 20, 45

Ophüls, Max, 4, 81
Ordet (Dreyer), 5, 21, 28-29, 36, 86
Orson Welles' Sketch Book (TV), 52
O'Toole, Fintan, 7
Out 1 (Rivette), 49, 62, 104
Out of the Past (Tourneur), 29
Ozep, Fedor, 40
Ozu, Yasujirō, 67-71

Paisan (Rossellini), 101
Palm, Michael, 54
Panahi, Jafar, 53
Paquin, Anna, 39
Paris nous appartient (Rivette), 49, 62
Passenger, The (Antonioni), 88-95
Passion of Joan of Arc, The, 86
Pipolo, Tony, 7
Phạm, Thiên Ân, 35-36, 94
Piccoli, Michel, 100
Phantom (Murnau), 59
Plaisir, Le (Ophüls), 81
Player, The (Altman), 65
Playhouse 90 (TV), 50-51
Portabella, Pere, 111-115
Presents (Snow), 88
Proust, Marcel, 75
Providence (Resnais), 14, 53, 76
Pudovkin, Vsevolod, 101, 108
Pylon (Faulkner), 2, 42-43, 89
Pynchon, Thomas, 33

Que Viva Mexico (Eisenstein), 101, 108

Ray, Nicholas, 51, 68
Rebecca (Hitchcock), 14
Red Desert (Antonioni), 93
Région centrale, La (Snow), 88
Richie, Donald, 69
Riefenstahl, Leni, 37-38
Renoir, Jean, 4, 41, 43, 97, 99
Resnais, Alain, 14, 31-32, 53, 73-83
Reverse Shot, 114
Rivette, Jacques, 41, 49, 62, 73-74
Robbe-Grillet, Alain, 31
Rooney, Mickey, 50
Rope (Hitchcock), 22
Rose, Reginald, 50
Rosenbaum, Stanley, 6

Rossellini, Roberto, 101
Rózsa, Miklós, 14
Rud, Ann Elisabeth, 86
Rye, Preben Lerdorff, 86

Sabu, 38
Sanctuary (Faulkner), 89
Saeed-Vafa, Mehrnaz, 6
Santos, Carles, 113, 115
Sátántangó (Tarr), 34
Sátántangó (Krasznahorkai), 34
Schaffner, Franklin J., 50
Schlagnitweit, Regina, 54
Schneider, Maria, 92
Schrader, Paul, 21
Scorsese, Martin, 101
See You Friday, Robinson (Farahani), 82
Serling, Rod, 50
Sembène, Ousmane, 81-82
Sesonske, Alexander, 42
Seyrig, Delphine, 31
Shakespeare, William, 8
Shannon, Harry, 85
Shining, The (Kubrick), 21
Sight and Sound, 21
Silence Before Bach, The (Portabella), 115
Sinatra, Frank, 47
Sirk, Douglas, 42-46
Snow, Michael, 87
Sondheim, Stephen, 82
Spielberg, Steven, 12
Star Wars (Lucas), 10
Statues Also Die (Resnais et al.), 77, 81
Stavisky (Resnais), 81-82
Sten, Anna, 40
Stephens, Bret, 11
Stewart, James, 21
Stoker, Bram, 113
Story of the Last Chrysanthemums, The (Mizoguchi), 70
Studio One (TV), 50-52
Sullivan, Ed, 11
Summer Storm (Sirk), 43
Sunrise (Murnau), 23-26, 81
Szirtes, George, 34

Tarantino, Michael, 63
Tarantino, Quentin, 64
Tarnished Angels, The (Sirk), 42-43, 45-46
Tarkovsky, Andrei, 4, 101
Tarr, Béla, 4, 34
Taubin, Amy, 87
Terry and the Pirates (Caniff), 80
That Night's Wife (Ozu), 68-71
Thief of Bagdad, The (Powell et al.), 38
Thing, The (Nyby), 45
Thomas, François, 80
Thunder on the Hill (Sirk), 42
Tonight Show, The (TV), 10
Touch of Evil (Welles), 102
Tourneur, Jacques, 29
Trente Ans avec Alain Resnais: Entretiens (Thomas), 80
Trial, The (Kafka), 47, 102
Trial, The (Welles), 76
Triumph of the Will (Riefenstahl), 38

Ulysses (Joyce), 47
Umbracle (Portabella), 115
Urusevsky, Sergei, 101, 103, 109

Vampir (Portabella), 115
Vampyr (Dreyer), 29, 86
Van Gogh (Resnais), 74
Vertigo (Hitchcock), 21
Vertov, Dziga, 36
Vierny, Sacha, 6
Vigo, Jean, 37
Village Voice, The, 111
Viridiana (Buñuel), 115
Vitti, Monica, 93-94
Von Harbou, Thea, 59
von Sternberg, Josef, 68

Warm, Hermann
War of the World, The (Welles), 48
Warsaw Bridge (Portabella), 115
Warshow, Robert, 108
Wavelength (Snow), 87-88
Weekend (Godard), 81-82
Weerasethakul, Apichatpong, 4
Welles, Orson, 4, 30, 48, 52-53, 76, 81, 83, 85, 10-102, 109
Wild Grass (Resnais), 77

Wind Across the Everglades (Ray), 30
Wright, Frank Lloyd, 6, 68
Written on the Wind (Sirk), 30, 42

Yevtushenko, Yevgeny, 101, 109
Yutkevich, Sergei, 102

Z (Costa-Gavras), 104
Zabriskie Point (Antonioni), 91, 93